Resilient Me

How to worry less and achieve more

Sam Owen

S

First published in Great Britain in 2017 by Orion Spring
an imprint of The Orion Publishing Group Ltd
Carmelite House, 50 Victoria Embankment
London EC4Y 0DZ
An Hachette UK Company

1 3 5 7 9 10 8 6 4 2

A CIP catalogue record for this book is
available from the British Library.

ISBN (Trade Paperback) 978 1 4091 7136 2
ISBN (eBook) 978 1 4091 7137 9

Every effort has been made to ensure that the information in the book is
accurate. The information in this book may not be applicable in each
individual case so it is advised that professional medical advice is
obtained for specific health matters and before changing any medication or
dosage. Neither the publisher nor author accepts any legal responsibility
for any personal injury or other damage or loss arising from the use of
the information in this book. In addition if you are concerned about your
diet or exercise regime and wish to change them, you should consult a
health practitioner first.

Printed and bound by CPI Group (UK) Ltd, Croydon, CR0 4YY

MIX
Paper from
responsible sources
FSC® C104740

www.orionbooks.co.uk

ORION
SPRING

This book is dedicated to my wonderful parents, beloved husband, the rest of my loving family and my dear friends. You are what makes life worth living.

Contents

Part 1:

Resilient Me Starts with Me

Resilience is Part of
Our Everyday Lives

'Life's ups and downs provide windows of opportunity to determine your values and goals. Think of using all obstacles as stepping stones to build the life you want.' Marsha Sinetar

Jenna knows that she wants to spend her life with someone but she is starting to worry that she will never find her Mr Right. After her fifth bad date this month, she is really starting to question herself (her worth, her personality and her abilities), and her faith that she'll achieve her goals of marriage and children is waning. Every unsuccessful date she goes on weighs her down more and more. Recently, she is increasingly walking around with her head down, shoulders hunched over and a slight frown on her face. She not only feels miserable, she's also starting to look it.

Chris, on the other hand, is a hard-working person but lately his boss has been regularly increasing his workload and criticising him more often than ever before. Chris is feeling overwhelmed, overworked and under-appreciated. When Chris's boss vents his anger over a project that was handed to Chris to complete, Chris leaves his boss's office questioning his ability to do the work and to cope with the pressures of his role. In their fast-paced, constantly evolving industry he needs to be able to roll with the punches and change direction with just a moment's notice, but recently he just hasn't felt as pliable and emotionally strong as he used to.

Whilst Jenna and Chris have their resilience chipped away from time to time as they struggle with the day-to-day stuff, there are also people like Sharon and Eddie, who are facing major life change and intense grief that requires them to maintain or rebuild their resilience after the massive dent or hole those big life traumas or tragedies create.

Sharon loves her job and has been progressively working towards career success her entire adult life, but one visit to the doctors reveals that the future she had envisioned for herself has been taken away. The life she had been excitedly working towards was almost over and she felt sick to her stomach. Sharon barely heard much else of what the doctor said as she sat there in disbelief. Weighed down by anxiety, she just about remembers walking back to her car, but barely remembers the drive home. She sits in her living room, in utter shock, tears streaming down her face.

Across town we have Eddie, husband to Gina and father to Sean and Sally. Eddie's world is turned upside down when Gina announces the marriage is truly over and wants them to start divorce proceedings. They had spoken about seeing a professional for some sort of marriage therapy but Eddie hadn't heeded Gina's many requests. Hearing his family and world are about to be torn apart, Eddie goes silent as he stands there in shock, but Gina sees his lack of overt emotional response as another sign of Eddie's apathy towards his family.

In life, we are faced with challenges that require resilience; those challenges may be like those that Jenna, Chris, Sharon and Eddie are facing. Other times, resilience is what we need for the moment-to-moment stuff, like when we spill a drink down the front of our clothes when we're running late for an appointment, or our kids aren't listening to us – again – and we feel as if we're failing as a parent.

Resilience is mental toughness that is at the same time mental flexibility to the changing winds of life. Like bamboo bending in the wind rather than snapping, resilience allows us to bend and ultimately stay upright and intact, rather than break and collapse in the face of life's challenges.

'Resilient people' understand that life will challenge them, sometimes in unexpected ways, sometimes in painful ways, but they relentlessly fight to overcome the challenge, whilst also welcoming lessons along the way.

'Non-resilient people', on the other hand, allow challenges to overcome them emotionally; they become fearful and anxious about their future (the next minute or the rest of their lives) and allow this fear and anxiety to take over. When we let fear and anxiety take over, we either become inactive or take action in the wrong direction.

Resilient people take control of themselves and the challenge; non-resilient people absolve themselves of control and let the challenge take control of them. Remember this: you are in charge of your life; not the universe, not your parents, spouse, boss or employees. You. Resilience requires you to take responsibility for your life and you have clearly assumed this responsibility by picking up this book.

Something brought you here to this book and, like many of my clients, it's often the point at which we feel enough is enough that we decide to do something about it. Maybe you're feeling bewildered, fed up and exhausted or can see yourself getting to that point quite soon. Maybe you feel as though life is out of your control and that no matter what you seem to do, nothing seems to go the way you want it to. Maybe you're worried that some important life goals seem to be getting further away from you, even though you would expect them to be within your reach by now. Whatever you're feeling, be proud of yourself for picking up this book. I'm proud of you. It takes a real winner to say, 'I'm going to do something about this and I know it's going to take work, but I will do it!'

By the end of this book you will know how to:

◊ feel strong, flexible and ready in the face of challenges, however traumatic, however unexpected;

◊ face challenges with optimism and even excitement;
◊ instantly engage a problem-solving mindset and approach;
◊ relentlessly problem-solve until you successfully overcome your challenges;
◊ quickly turn negative emotions into positive emotions;
◊ maintain consistent mental well-being on the whole;
◊ surround yourself with people who reinforce your resilience;
◊ ultimately achieve all the goals that you have a burning desire to achieve.

Resilience is about Survival

Resilience is when the unwelcome happens and we find a way to 'roll with the punches' and overcome heartache or obstacles. Resilience is when the unexpected happens but we keep our nerve and handle whatever challenge is resting in our lap. Resilience is when the unthinkable happens and we keep faith, trusting that after the storm will again come the calm. Resilience is when we are relentless in our search for an alternative way to keep moving in the direction we want to go in or have faith that the forced reroute brings benefits of some sort.

When we think of human resilience, we might think of words like toughness and flexibility, and how quickly and easily a person overcomes challenges, big and small, and keeps moving forward in life, achieving goals along the way. When we think of a community's resilience, we might think of how quickly and easily it rebuilds itself after the havoc wreaked by a natural disaster such as an earthquake. When we think of a failing company's resilience, we may think of how quickly and easily it manages change and builds a successful empire once again. Resilience is everywhere. You experience it daily in others and in yourself. It's that inner, flexible tough guy or girl that raises his or her head with passion and says, 'I can handle it!' and 'I can do this!' Resilience allows you to keep powering forward in life despite all the challenges along the way, big and small.

Resilience is necessary for our physical survival, for our mental and physical well-being, for our ability to realise our potential, and for the successful achievement of our life goals. At a basic, primitive level, our primary goal as humans is physical survival; the avoidance of death for as long as possible despite its inevitability. Resilience is vital for our survival, both as individual human beings and as a species. In ancient times, resilience would have been required to fend off much more overt dangers like being mauled to death by an animal whilst out hunting for food. Imagine if, in those times when survival was the order of the day, a man stood frozen with fear upon seeing a predator appear in front of him. Regardless of whether that man was expecting to encounter such a threat during that hunting trip, he would need to keep his nerve and either fight the animal or flee from it. They would be the only survival options available to him. Without a can-do attitude and quick problem-solving followed by quick action, that man would be dead. In the modern day we are still fighting for our survival but now our needs are simply more sophisticated, even though they still ultimately serve to keep us alive. Modern survival means having enough money for fuel, clothing and shelter; thoughtfully looking after our bodies well enough to stave off life-threatening illness; fulfilling our potential in order to easily maintain emotional well-being which, in addition to making life worth living, directly and indirectly affects our ability to achieve our basic survival needs for fuel, clothing and shelter; and creating a family or social network to keep us feeling valued and, as research suggests, enabling a longer lifespan.

The Definition of Resilience

A good definition of human resilience is: **the ability to recover quickly from life's setbacks**.

In other words, resilience depends upon the **manner** and **speed** with which we cope with difficulties:

◊ the manner being the way we inwardly and outwardly conduct ourselves whenever faced with a challenge;
◊ the speed being how quickly we charge forwards from the moment the challenge has been encountered to the moment the end goal has been achieved.

If resilience depends upon the manner and speed with which we cope with difficulties, what determines our manner and our speed each time we have to call upon our internal resource of resilience?

Having successfully helped many coaching clients with their relationships, anxiety, self-esteem, confidence and life direction, I have encountered feats of resilience on all points of the spectrum, from the small stuff to the big challenges.

On the one end of the spectrum I've had clients who have taken challenges in their stride, always thinking in terms of what they have learnt so that they can put the lessons to use in order to achieve their goals. On the extreme opposite end of the spectrum I've seen clients treat every challenge as a misfortune and get stuck in negative emotions and inaction. Some of these clients move along the spectrum to the resilient, lesson-embracing end after a few sessions; those on antidepressants usually require a few more sessions before they move in this direction; and very occasionally I have witnessed those who have simply refused to undertake simple coaching tasks that would have moved them closer towards their goals. There are clear, distinct patterns that differentiate the resilient clients from their less resilient counterparts, as we will uncover.

This book is the culmination of all that I have learnt through coaching, the research I have read that supports how I have seen my clients feel, behave and achieve, and the research I have read that backs up the techniques I've successfully used with coaching clients, time and time again.

So let's find out how we can develop and maintain resilience so that we bounce over obstacles with ease every time life challenges us!

The Three Pillars of Resilience

*'Every adversity, every failure, every heartache carries
with it the seed of an equal or greater benefit.'*
Napoleon Hill

Some people seem to have personalities that naturally lend
themselves to resilience, whilst others have been forced to exercise
their 'resilience muscle' a great deal during their lifetime and are
now experienced at it. Whether we've been highly resilient in the
past or not, we can *all* build our resilience through practice.

What determines our manner and speed each time we have to
practise resilience is comprised of what I have termed the **Three
Pillars of Resilience**. These three pillars constitute the necessary
foundation of all human resilience.

Very briefly, the Three Pillars of Resilience are:

A. A **positive outlook** on challenges
B. A **driving motivation** to achieve the end goal
C. A **problem-solving** approach

That's it! These three pillars will enable you to immediately
experience the 'resilient you'. The four-week resilience plan will
allow you to train your brain and body to habitually handle challenges with immediate resilience, fairly subconsciously, without
you thinking about it a great deal – much like brushing your teeth.

Remember, anything we do repeatedly becomes a habit as the
brain and body become used to executing it. When something

becomes a habit, we are able to do it with little thought and little effort. Repetitively doing something is in fact so powerful that we sometimes form habits without any intention, like when a person's accent changes when they start living in a different city. Of course, other times we form habits with intention because we know they are good habits that will help us, like getting enough sleep each night and facing challenges with resilience.

Until recently, we have been predominantly led to believe that long-standing mental health or personal problems require difficult solutions and/or a long time to fix. There is a whole industry that has benefited from this belief even though many of those working within it are as innocent as the rest of us, as they too were socialised just as we were. Yet I have helped the vast majority of my clients achieve their goals, or be well on their way to doing so, in just three to eight sixty-minute coaching sessions; many in just three. Some of these clients resolved chronic anxiety or lack of confidence in just two to three coaching sessions. Some clients have even transformed low self-esteem in as little as three coaching sessions. Some couples have addressed long-standing problems and averted potential divorce, after just three coaching sessions. One client, Natalie T, overcame chronic OCD that had plagued her for roughly thirty years since about the age of eight, after just three coaching sessions.

From the day my practice began I have watched my clients prove time and time again that changing even the most chronic, long-standing, painful situations takes relatively little time and effort when the Three Pillars of Resilience are in place.

The simplest solutions are usually the most powerful and when my clients understand both how their brain and body function, and why – based on research and common sense – they can achieve seeming miracles in their life in astoundingly little time!

So that you can do the same, we'll explore each pillar before moving on to the strategies that protect the Three Pillars from erosion and enhance their strength, enabling you to build and maintain the new, resilient you in four weeks or less!

For now, just sit back, relax, take in everything you read, enjoy the research and case studies, and make sure you do all the 'Over To You' exercises so that when you have finished the book, you are ready to start your four-week resilience plan. Keep all written exercises in one place, along with a note of any epiphanies you have. This way, when you reach the end of the book, you have everything to hand to start your uber simple four-week plan.

Resilience Pillar 1 – A Positive Outlook on Challenges

Resilience starts in the mind and it stems from our outlook on life's challenges: it's how we choose to view our challenges.

For centuries, philosophers, psychologists and leaders have asserted that it is the way we evaluate what happens, not what happens, that determines our emotions and our behaviours. In other words, the thoughts we attach to events, whether in the privacy of our mind or outwardly as spoken words, determine four things: how we feel, how we behave, the outcomes we achieve, and other thoughts we have. Underpinning the success of coaching and Cognitive Behavioural Therapy (CBT) alike is this influential link between how people think, feel and behave and the outcomes they then achieve.

Your outlook on life's challenges is how you think about them and that very outlook influences how you feel and behave whenever faced with a challenge, the outcomes you achieve as a result of those emotions and behaviours, and other thoughts you have about yourself, the challenge, your goal, your future and so on.

You will find your current outlook on life's challenges either falls closer to the self-serving end of the spectrum or the self-sabotaging end of the spectrum, i.e. your outlook either serves you or sabotages you. Let's look at the self-serving end of the spectrum first.

On the furthest point of the self-serving end of the spectrum, resilient people have the positive outlook that life's challenges are:

◊ **events and lessons that guide us towards our goals, happiness and life purpose.**

For this reason, resilient people embrace challenges:

◊ **optimistically, thoughtfully and proactively.**

This positive outlook becomes self-serving because it produces outcomes like:

◊ **feeling grateful** for the challenge even if the benefits are yet unknown to us;
◊ **taking responsibility** for ourselves as we make use of any lessons and other benefits the challenge offers;
◊ **having self-belief** that we can 'handle it' because we're feeling optimistic and are focused on finding solutions;
◊ **welcoming challenges** as they are seen as nudging us towards our goals and happiness.

On the furthest point of the self-sabotaging end of the spectrum, non-resilient people have the negative outlook that life's challenges are:

◊ **unfortunate events that block us from our goals, happiness and life purpose.**

For this reason, non-resilient people recoil from challenges:

◊ **pessimistically, without thinking clearly and without taking actions that will truly help them.**

This negative outlook becomes self-sabotaging because it produces outcomes like:

◊ **viewing ourselves as victims** of the challenge even if the 'cost' is yet unknown;
◊ **lacking responsibility** for our own life because we don't view the challenge as a source of learning, personal growth and other benefits;
◊ **having self-doubt** about whether we can 'handle it' because we're feeling pessimistic, and are more focused on self-pity than on finding solutions;
◊ **evaluating challenges as unnecessary and unwelcome** as they are seen as blocking us from our goals and happiness.

When I see clients with a self-sabotaging negative outlook on challenges, I notice them panic as they make assumptions that their challenges are a negative sign that their goal won't happen, or worse, that they are not worthy of their goal.

On the other hand, I notice clients with a self-serving positive outlook on challenges identify that they are getting stuck somewhere and want my help figuring out where, uncovering lessons and benefits and helping to put them to good use.

You see, the self-serving positive outlook doesn't stop the experience of emotional pain; it accepts the pain but simply goes two steps further than the self-sabotaging negative outlook, which just gets stuck in the pain. The self-serving positive outlook allows us to frame the situation positively and use the experience as a feedback loop – a source of information which then allows us to reorganise our actions in the direction of our goals.

Remember that even when we are resiliently facing a challenge:

◊ sometimes the benefits are immediate and we are immediately aware of them;

◊ other times the benefits are long-term but we are still
   immediately aware of them;
◊ other times the benefits are immediate but we only become
   aware of them later on;
◊ other times the benefits are long-term and we only become
   aware of them further along life's journey.

In other words, whether the lessons and other benefits are immediate or long-term and whether we are immediately aware of
them or not, they are there for those looking for them and if you
search, you will eventually find them.

Your outlook dictates whether you search for the lessons
and benefits or not, and in this way one might say that a
self-sabotaging outlook creates a 'blind spot' because by
neglecting to look for lessons and benefits we block ourselves
from seeing the full picture. A self-serving outlook does not have
a blind spot because we move our perspective as we search for the
lessons and other benefits. With the self-sabotaging outlook we
do not even try to move our perspective because we think we
have no reason to . . .

So we each have a choice: embrace an outlook that cultivates
resilience and sounds more realistic when we think about life from
the perspective of mankind/human beings in general, rather than
solely based on our life experience so far, or embrace one that will
unnerve us and sabotage our own goals and happiness.

Our chosen outlook on life's challenges determines how
resilient we are because our thoughts influence our emotions and
behaviours, and thus the outcomes we achieve, whether intentional
or accidental. This is how your mind materialises things into your
life. What we think determines the direction we steer our brain
and body in. **One might see thoughts as influencing the
direction in which we steer our life.**

Words Shape Our Experience of an Experience

It's not what happens that matters; it's how we think about it. Let's use a silly example to really drive the point home that our thoughts influence our life, so that you then get behind the steering wheel of your life by taking control of your thoughts. Imagine for a moment that you think all cats are highly dangerous animals:

◊ Would you avoid domesticated cats in close proximity to you?
◊ Would you experience anxiety and/or fear when you were near domesticated cats?
◊ If you were dining outdoors in the summer, would you struggle to enjoy your meal if a neighbour's cat kept wandering about by your table?

Of course you will have answered yes, yes, and yes because you intuitively know that these would be natural reactions if you viewed all cats as highly dangerous animals. In your mind, your safety is being threatened even if in reality it isn't.

Is the reality shaping your reaction in this scenario or your thoughts? Your thoughts: because the reality is that all cats are not highly dangerous animals but if your personal outlook states that they are, you will respond accordingly, regardless of the reality.

Outlook Scenario 1 (Negative = Self-Sabotaging)

Now imagine for a moment that your outlook is that **life's challenges are unfortunate events that block us from our goals, happiness and life purpose** and the career promotion you have been working towards for the last ten months has been given to someone else:

◊ Name two emotions you might experience, e.g. sadness, fear, anger, bewilderment, frustration.
◊ Name two behaviours you might subsequently indulge as a result of those emotions.
◊ Name two possible outcomes of those subsequent behaviours.

You might have come up with something similar to these, given your negative outlook on challenges in this scenario:

◊ Two possible emotions: sadness and anger.
◊ Two possible resulting behaviours: being rude to your boss and consuming lots of alcohol to numb the negative emotions.
◊ Possible outcomes of these resulting behaviours: damaging your relationship with your boss, feeling somewhat depressed and foggy-headed in the mornings, and gaining weight from your heavy alcohol consumption.
◊ Possible long-term consequences: your depressed moods and alcohol-related grogginess resulting in poorer performance at work, in turn making you feel undeserving of the job in the first place, making it less likely you will get a promotion in future.

These outcomes then feed back into your thought processes about your boss, your job, yourself, and your career goals.

These outcomes also feed back into your outlook on challenges, reinforcing it: 'See, life *is* always against me; whatever I do is never enough; I am so unlucky; it's so unfair; bad things always happen to me.'

Outlook Scenario 2 (Positive = Self-Serving)

Now imagine the same scenario – the career promotion you have been working towards for the last ten months has been given to someone else – but this time imagine your outlook is that **life's challenges are events and lessons that guide us towards our goals, happiness and life purpose**. In naming possible emotions, behaviours, direct outcomes and long-term consequences of that outlook, you might come up with something like this:

◊ Two possible emotions: surprise and intrigue.
◊ Two possible resulting behaviours: learning new skills to help you achieve the promotion next time, or actively reassessing if this is the right career path for you and proactively exploring alternative career options.
◊ Two possible outcomes of these resulting behaviours: becoming more skilled and confident and getting offered an even better promotion a few months later, or pursuing a lifelong hobby as a new career instead.
◊ Long-term possible consequences: going on to have a fulfilling career and achieving other important life goals with your developed self-belief.

These outcomes then feed back into your thought processes about your boss, your job, yourself, your career goals and more.

These outcomes also feed back into your outlook on challenges, reinforcing it: 'Everything happens for the best in the end, even when I can't understand why straight away; even when the experience is painful, I always end up with a happier, more fulfilling life.'

Although we choose our outlook on challenges based on what feels like 'common sense' as we think about life, we must remember that – as demonstrated by the simple examples above – we will find and create proof of our chosen outlook, regardless of which one we choose. Our outlook on life's challenges becomes a self-fulfilling prophecy because it influences what we feel, do, achieve and then think again, whether it is setting us up at an advantage or disadvantage, or setting us up for success or failure.

Your outlook to date has been serving as a self-fulfilling prophecy and it is partially responsible for where your life is right now. Whichever outlook you choose from this point on will also serve as a self-fulfilling prophecy, either in a self-serving way or a self-sabotaging way.

I appreciate that changing your outlook may feel superficial at first, but as you get behind it and have some fun playing with it, watching how changing your outlook alters your emotions and behaviours, you'll see how it affects the immediate and long-term outcomes you achieve.

Choose your outlook based on intelligent, reflective thought, not based on what you have experienced to date, because your experience so far has been shaped by your thoughts and outlooks, which may have been self-sabotaging.

When we choose a self-serving, positive outlook on life's challenges, it helps us to achieve our goals, happiness and life purpose. It also directly and indirectly influences the happiness of our loved ones, colleagues and mankind as the effects of how we think, feel and behave radiate out towards our fellow humans.

Resilience Pillar 2 – A Driving Motivation to Achieve the End Goal

Resilience also comes from a driving motivation to (a) stay alive; the survival goal, and (b) achieve our life goals.

In the first instance, we have to be motivated to stay alive. Some people don't feel motivated to live any longer because they are suffering dearly, either emotionally or physically. They may be willing death to come and take them, asking loved ones for euthanasia, or considering suicide. Think of the poor child who tries to commit suicide because of relentless school bullying, or the ageing father with the excruciatingly painful terminal illness, or the mother who lost all her family in a house fire.

These people can still have a change of heart and decide they do want to stay alive, and do so because they change their outlook on life's challenges to become a self-serving positive one (Resilience Pillar 1). In other words, Resilience Pillar 1 (a positive outlook on challenges) can pave the way to Resilience Pillar 2 (a driving motivation to achieve the end goal). For example, the mother who lost her family in the fire may decide to make it her life's purpose to educate people on fire hazards in the home, thereby preventing others from experiencing the same distressing loss she has suffered. Notice how changing our outlook gives us a different perspective on what has happened to us in life and why, and can thus motivate us to want to stay alive and do something with the experience we have been given. Often, when we find meaning, we find strength and purpose.

Similarly to staying alive, we have to be motivated to achieve our life goals because if we're not truly motivated to achieve a particular goal (big or small) we won't put the effort in to achieve it. We may even look for excuses to move us away from it, even if inaction and excuses are subconsciously motivated.

Sometimes our subconscious mind (working in the background) knows before our conscious mind does that we don't really want to pursue a particular goal, even if we're consciously telling ourselves and others around us that we do. I see this happening all the time with my clients.

I remember Caroline M, an HR manager, who told me her number-one goal was to write a book, only to find that she wasn't making progress on finishing her manuscript and hadn't been for some time. When she came to me she was tentative about embarking upon coaching and was also feeling very apathetic in life. What transpired during our four coaching sessions was that this book goal was actually a little further down Caroline's list of priorities: at number three. Only once she had identified and started to make progress on her number-one and -two goals, which were expanding her social circle and finding her Mr Right, did she start making progress again on her unfinished novel. It was as though her subconscious mind was saying, 'Before you prioritise and focus your time and energy on your book goal, you need to identify, prioritise and focus your time and energy on your true primary goals'. Caroline, soon after identifying her true primary goals, started to make simple changes that made her feel in control of her life, happier day-to-day and open to new experiences. She started taking bold steps towards her goals, began a fantastic relationship with her Mr Right and eventually finished her manuscript, too! Caroline and Mr Right are still together three years later and still very much in love.

When we lack true motivation to achieve something, it can be for a number of reasons. For example:

◊ Having different priorities from those consciously identified.

◊ Conflicting goals seem mutually exclusive ('I can't possibly have this and that').

◊ Crippling lack of self-belief ('I don't believe I can do this so I am not even motivated to try').

◊ Not knowing what your goals are ('I'm not sure what I want to achieve').

◊ Falsely, albeit unknowingly, adopting other people's goals as your own goals ('I too want to complete a marathon').

◊ Working towards goals others expect you to achieve even though they're not your goals ('I'll go for the promotion, even though I don't want to, just to give my family more disposable income').

So if you're feeling stuck or like a failure or a procrastinator, maybe it's just that your 'goal' isn't really your goal, or at least, not one that you're that motivated to achieve. If you can easily live without a thing, you probably won't achieve it if the road to success has obstacles because Resilience Pillar 2 – a driving motivation to achieve the end goal – will be missing.

Instead of judging yourself negatively, only study yourself as we go through every chapter of this book. Judgements aren't necessary; being a student of your own life is. It's incredibly empowering to really know what your goals are and what motivates you. It becomes a clear, driving force in your life that makes everything fall into place, effortlessly. It makes decisions simple, even the toughest times manageable, and energy is in easy supply.

Being a student of your own life is so empowering because it says, 'I am in charge; I constantly learn about myself and just tweak the things that need tweaking!' Plus, because using this approach will move you towards your goals and happiness, you'll have fun! No one ever complained about achieving their goals and feeling happier and excited about life!

⊨ OVER TO YOU ⊨

A) Right now, create and complete a table like this with as many rows as you need:

Important life goal	Do I have a driving motivation to achieve it?	If so, why am I motivated to achieve it?

Your answers may change as you go through this book and become increasingly self-aware and proactive. That's fine! Some goals you'll realise are not so important to you right now but may be later, e.g. having children. Other goals you may feel are nice-to-haves but you have zero motivation for putting in the effort required, e.g. completing a marathon. You definitely don't want to weigh yourself down or distract yourself from your important life goals with goals you're not genuinely motivated to achieve.

B) Using this table, create (and edit as required going forward) a written list of your ultimate specific goals, with a specific date for achieving them by (however odd or difficult that may seem to you right now).

C) Review the list daily if you can, but at least weekly. It's very important to keep your goals at the forefront of your mind, as you will see.

Resilience Pillar 3 – A Problem-Solving Approach

Once Resilience Pillars 1 and 2 have been satisfied, i.e. we have (1) a positive outlook on challenges, and (2) a driving motivation to achieve the end goal, there is just one pillar left to build for reso-lute resilience to exist. When resilience is required, we must always problem-solve whatever challenge we are facing.

Overcoming a challenge often requires that we gain knowledge, overcome fears, create a plan of action, remove removable obstacles, find a way around immovable obstacles, gain cooperation from others, invest money in something, (e.g. technology, clothing, yoga), and invest our time in learning something necessary (e.g. knowledge about a topic, a new skill, a new way of thinking). To date, you have already done this many times over. Think about that right now.

⊨ OVER TO YOU ⊨

Recall a difficult time in your life when at least one obstacle stood in the way of a goal that you just *had* to achieve. In one sentence, what did you do to overcome that goal? Finish this sentence: 'I . . . and thus achieved my important goal as a result.'

As you just *had* to achieve it, you noted any obstacles and you did what you had to in order to overcome them. Simple. You found a way.

⊨

Programming Your 'Sat-Nav' so you can do the Problem-Solving

In life, we have to be able to problem-solve life's challenges and the better at it we are, the less emotional stress we experience. Negative emotions can trigger the fight-or-flight response, whilst identifying negative emotions with the correct word label diminishes the fight-or-flight response and simultaneously engages a section within the brain region associated with 'executive function' like reasoning, planning and problem-solving.[1] By being aware of the exact negative emotion we are experiencing, rather than simply being at the mercy of it, our brain seems able to dissipate our instinctive, defensive response, allowing us to move onto thoughtful problem-solving instead.

Interestingly, Charles Kettering, the man who invented the starter motor for cars, once said, 'A problem well-stated is a problem half-solved.' It appears the brain may think the same way!

⊨ OVER TO YOU ⊨

When I have clients who are getting stuck in negative emotions rather than moving on towards problem-solving, here's what I suggest to them and you should do it too, every time you get stuck in negative emotions and a problem focus.

- Identify the negative emotions you are experiencing by writing them down on a notepad, typing them into your phone, or just having a word with yourself. Finish the sentence by correctly labelling the negative emotions: 'I am feeling . . .'
- As you identify your negative emotions correctly, notice how your body starts to feel more relaxed as the tension begins to dissipate and the fight-or-flight response diminishes.
- Smile and take a sigh of relief, because by identifying the negative emotions you are experiencing, you learn your starting point (A), i.e. where you are right now.
- Next, identify your destination (B). Write down or vocalise the positive emotions you would rather experience. Finish the sentence using the positive emotions you desire: 'I want to feel . . .'

You can now begin problem-solving what you need to do to get from A to B (as Resilience Pillar 3 is the use of a problem-solving approach). Think of it as programming your brain's 'sat-nav' so that your brain can find the best route for you.

━━━━┥

Rewiring Your Brain for Resilience in Four Weeks or Less,
Using the Three Pillars

The human brain is always evolving to meet new challenges and adapt to our ever-changing world. Neuroscientists refer to this as 'neuroplasticity' because the brain can be reshaped and remoulded, and does so right into old age. This 'plasticity' allows us to create new habits, and break old ones, by changing the physical structure of our brain. In basic terms, two things that consistently and repeatedly occur simultaneously become linked together in your brain as though one always occurs with the other, purely because this is how your brain has consistently and repeatedly experienced them. If you always experience optimism and happiness in the presence of a certain friend, your brain comes to associate that friend with those two emotions. If you always hold the phone in your left hand, your brain will expect and propel you to pick up the phone with your left hand when it rings. These links we've created can induce immediate associations in our thoughts, give rise to associated emotions and propel us to indulge certain behaviours, often automatically. During most of your day you do things that your brain has established neural pathways for and so it bypasses your conscious thinking and instead makes you just – do it.

When we do something new we create a new pathway in the brain. One might think of this as a dusty road off the beaten track. When we repeat something over and over to the point of it becoming a habit, the brain will have travelled that pathway many times over and, the once dusty side-road becomes an established highway. Thereafter, it is so much easier for the brain to travel down the now well-trodden path that it begins to do so somewhat automatically, often with little thought required. That's why habits are easy to create through repetition and breaking them simply means not taking those established roads for long enough that they diminish through lack of use (see page 69). So if you think resilience feels alien to you, it's just that you have yet to create those established pathways in your brain. You will learn how to do this, easily, as you progress through this book. The brain's physical structure is influenced by our thoughts, emotions and behaviours, and so we can let the brain remould itself by leaving it on auto-pilot or we can take control and purposefully remould it ourselves for the habits that are going to serve us . . . like resilience. **This is how you achieve resilience in four weeks or less:** you remould your brain for resilience so that it becomes a habit. When something becomes a habit, we indulge that habit with little conscious effort. It is easy for the brain to do something it has already done many times over, and by repeating the habit, we naturally maintain it, easily.

Yep, you can change whether you are resilient or not, and record that new version of yourself into your brain, simply through repeatedly honouring the Three Pillars of Resilience.

I successfully use habit-breaking and 'habit-wiring' techniques in my work with self-esteem clients, confidence clients, anxiety clients, dating clients, couples clients, weight-loss clients, depressed clients and more. When clients take charge of how they are shaping their brain, they start making speedy progress on their mental health, their relationships and their goals. Neuroplasticity is how we change our view of ourselves (our self-image), how we get better at performing a task, how we create good habits in our life and how we break bad, self-sabotaging habits that aren't serving us. Thankfully we are not hard-wired and stuck with the current brain we have. Just like you change your body through training and exercise or lack thereof, you change your brain through training and exercise or lack thereof, whether you choose to be at the helm or not. More on this as we go through the book, and I'll show you how to do this for yourself.

That Classic Dog Experiment

At the start of the twentieth century, physiologist Ivan Pavlov conducted an experiment with dogs. Pavlov consistently and repeatedly presented dogs with a plate of food whilst at the same time sounding a metronome. When he did so, the dogs would salivate at the sight of the food. He then discovered that if he later sounded the metronome on its own, without presenting food, the dogs would still salivate at the mere sound of the metronome. After Pavlov had consistently and repeatedly sounded the metronome whilst presenting food, the dogs' brains had come to associate the sound of the metronome with the presence of food. Pavlov and his dogs demonstrated over a century ago how we physically 'wire' habits into our brain. In the same way, we are going to get your brain to eventually associate you with resilience.

Why Resilience has Historically been a Challenge for Some

'Obstacles, of course, are developmentally necessary:
they teach kids strategy, patience, critical thinking,
resilience and resourcefulness.' Naomi Wolf

You are going to find that being resilient is easy when you honour the Three Pillars of Resilience:

1. A positive outlook on challenges
2. A driving motivation to achieve the end goal
3. A problem-solving approach

. . . and utilise the upcoming strategies to assist you.

If any one of these pillars is missing, resilience can be impossible to achieve. Before we further explore the Three Pillars and discuss the strategies for reinforcing them, let's look at some of the reasons why you may have struggled to develop your resilience in day-to-day life.

Why Some People Get Stuck

Often, people get stuck simply because they have a negative out-look on challenges. You can have a driving motivation to achieve your goal (Resilience Pillar 2 is present) but if you don't have a positive outlook on challenges (Resilience Pillar 1 is missing), you will not engage in proper problem-solving (Resilience Pillar 3 will be missing). After numerous attempts and perceived 'failures', stemming from the two missing pillars (1 and 3), you may view yourself as either incapable of overcoming a challenge and achieving the end goal or, worse, unworthy of achieving that end goal. Intriguingly, you can create a negative self-image purely by having a negative outlook on challenges.

Other times, people get stuck because of a fear of some sort, which hinders the presence of a driving motivation to achieve the end goal (Resilience Pillar 2 is missing). They want to move forward but something is stopping them. Or they get stuck because they do not know how to problem-solve challenges (Resilience Pillar 3 is missing) and so struggle to overcome them.

As you read through the following sections, make a mental note of which categories might apply to you.

A self-sabotaging self-image

We know from research that our self-image influences our behaviour. You may have already noticed this in everyday life. For example, people who believe they are poor at remembering names will blatantly fail to even try to remember a person's name when they first hear it. On the other hand, people who believe they are good at remembering names will immediately use a simple strategy for remembering it. Our self-image dictates whether we use self-serving and goal-serving behaviours or self-sabotaging and goal-sabotaging behaviours.

In a study on academically struggling school students with declining mathematics grades, researchers found that if they taught students that intelligence is malleable and can be developed with effort, their motivation and grades improved compared with students who were taught that intelligence is fixed.[2] For the students who were taught that intelligence is fixed, their grades continued to decline.

The researchers note that even when students had equal intelligence, their outlook on intelligence shaped how they responded to academic challenges. They discovered that students with the outlook that intelligence is changeable (a) set bigger goals for learning, (b) had more positive beliefs about actually putting effort into learning, and (c) made fewer 'helpless' judgements about not being capable. As a result, the students chose more positive, effort-based strategies to overcome their challenges, which boosted their mathematics grades over time.

In other words, whether you believe you can influence or control something determines whether you'll even try to and if you do, you'll put more effort and positivity into it.

If your current self-image is grounded in a **lack of self-belief** that you're capable of achieving an important goal, you won't properly try to achieve it, even though you may think you have been trying. An ongoing negative self-image will influence your behaviours to the point where you stop trying as hard and then sometimes stop trying to overcome challenges altogether. This can lead to a feeling of hopelessness and depression, clinical or unofficial. When working with clients who are on antidepressants, it becomes apparent that when they start better engaging with their thoughts through coaching, and look for lessons and other benefits of their painful experiences, they improve their self-image, feel more empowered, use better behaviours to try to overcome their challenges, and subsequently, start to come out of their depression. This also enables them to end their use of antidepressants.

If your current self-image is grounded in a **lack of self-worth**, you will not feel deserving of your goals and their good fortune. When I have clients like this, they incorrectly view themselves as less worthy of happiness than others. I particularly see this with some dating coaching clients who are starting to panic. They have decided, often through evaluation of their past 'failures', that perhaps the 'failures' represent them as fundamentally unlovable human beings or undeserving of their goal (to find Mr or Mrs Right to spend their life with). This is what can happen when Resilience Pillar 1 – a positive outlook on challenges – is not in place: panic, fear and a crumbling self-image.

I remember my client, Sarah J, repeatedly getting stuck each time a challenge to her resilience appeared. Every time she had a bad date, every time she felt scared about attending a social function to meet single guys, every time she struggled to find matches on online dating sites, every time the guy she liked didn't like her back, she would panic and feel upset. As it was for Sarah, it's important for you to recognise that how you have attempted to achieve your goals to date may be the reason for your 'failures' to date, but bears no relation to your worth as a human being. Slowly, through helping Sarah to shift her outlook on her dating challenges, this reactive panic started to shift towards more reflective thoughts and proactive behaviours.

As with clients like Sarah, I urge you to:

◊ draw a line under past experiences caused by a self-sabotaging negative outlook, which will have resulted in a self-sabotaging, flawed approach;

◊ **embrace a self-serving positive outlook and then use all challenges as a feedback loop, a source of knowledge** to help redirect your course to get back on track and ultimately achieve your goals.

As Resilience Pillar 1 states, if we have a positive outlook on challenges, then we can start to think about what the lessons and other benefits might be, for example: 'Could my approach have been better?', 'How might I do things differently from this point on?', 'Where would I find the solutions?' or in Sarah's case, 'Where would I find the sort of guy I would like to date?'

Your past does not define you unless you allow or want it to. Your past merely tells you the limits created by the outlook and strategies you employed back then. As we continue on this journey together, you are going to learn how to **shape your self-worth, daily**, how you can quickly change yours for the better as my clients do, and how to successfully achieve your goals.

If you haven't yet completed the previous tasks I've set within these pages, do them now and then come back here and continue reading.

Fear of change

Some people are so afraid of the unknown that they would rather stay where they are than experience a little uncertainty, and perhaps a little 'risk' to their self-esteem or confidence. The irony is, we build our self-esteem and confidence by having the guts to 'feel the fear and do it anyway', as Susan Jeffers once put it. Avoiding such opportunities for personal growth keeps us stuck in the self-image we have rather than giving us the chance to evolve and grow. Of course, that is easier said than done . . . or is it? (I say with a wink and a smile.)

If you are struggling with fear of change, here are a few simple solutions:

A. Remember that, most of the time, the discomfort we anticipate experiencing is nearly always greater than any discomfort we actually experience when we do the thing. You can test this for yourself by rating on a scale of one to ten (if ten is extremely) how uncomfortable or scary you think something is going to be prior to doing it and rating it again on the same scale afterwards to see how uncomfortable or scary it was in reality. You'll find you nearly always rate the reality lower on the scale than you previously thought. Furthermore, we often end up actually enjoying the experience instead, sometimes because it's fun, but sometimes because we prove our abilities to ourselves and improve our self-image, both of which can be exhilarating!

B. Minimise 'risks' or minimise the anxiety as best you can
   by preparing in minute detail for anything that causes
   you fear; also prevent any potential problems you can.
   For example, one client, Mary A, had severe social
   anxiety. She had been through a trauma and bit by bit
   she had retreated from life. Now, re-entering the outside
   world seemed too scary, however much she wanted to do
   it. Mary and I identified all the things that made her feel
   anxious about going out socially so that Mary could then
   minimise or eliminate those 'risks' altogether. She
   planned her outfits carefully, prepped answers to any
   unwelcome questions she expected others to ask,
   planned responses that would instantly stop any further
   unwelcome conversations in their tracks, and created exit
   strategies should she desperately want to leave a social
   event early. The outfits boosted her confidence, the
   prepped responses meant she felt ready for any awkward
   questions, and the exit strategy meant she rarely felt the
   need to use it but could relax knowing she could leave
   easily if she wanted to. You can do the same: plan and
   prepare for dreaded possibilities so that they are no
   longer dreaded.

C. Seek out a motivational quote or two to help you feel
   inspired or more confident, for example:
   ◊ 'Take the first step in faith. You don't have to see
     the whole staircase, just take the first step.' – Martin
     Luther King Jr
   ◊ 'Thinking will not overcome fear but action will.' –
     W. Clement Stone

Fear of success

Separate to a fear of failing, a fear of success can consist of a
number of fears. One is that we might lose 'friends' because they
begrudge our new-found success, whether that success is an

accolade, an increase in income, a gorgeous physique, or something else.

If we change our station in life, people's attitudes towards us may change. True, but the people who genuinely love us, care about us and want the best for us will be happy for our success. Your life may become a mirror in which they view their own lack of progress in life, but that mirror will help them if they love you and care about you. The people in your life that begrudge your success and happiness are not 'your people', so when they start to attack that mirror (you) because they don't like their own reflection, don't worry because they are not concerned about you, your success or your well-being.

There are also other fears that can come with success, for example: becoming vulnerable to jealous colleagues trying to sabotage your state of mind, or people wanting to put you down if you are a public figure, or realising that your partner or friends will get left behind if they do not personally grow and develop as you are doing. The solution is to surround yourself only with the people who truly care for you, and to do what you can to ensure your loved ones also pursue personal growth so that you can continue enjoying the journey of life together as you both continuously mature and develop.

Fear of losing current benefits

Brace yourself; this can be a tough pill to swallow. Some people go through life saying they want to change and improve life and become healthy, happy, slim, get off antidepressants, be more mobile, have fewer days of illness, have more fun and so on, but ... they don't really want those things. They prefer the perks that come with their 'unfortunate situation' even if there are elements of their current situation that they really dislike.

I had one client where I experienced this first-hand, even though she had pleaded I take her on as a client, and had promised she was ready to make positive changes in her life despite several previous unsuccessful attempts. She had discussed which perks she would lose and what sort of additional effort would be expected of her if she were to become well again. What caught my attention was how she would only smile when she could tell me that she didn't believe a strategy would work, or had found something 'hadn't helped'. It was the consistent timing of her subconscious smiles that eventually gave her inner motivations away within a few sessions. It's not that these people don't want to get better; it's just that they find their current perks more appealing than the 'costs' of the alternative life.

Fear of embarrassment if a theory or approach 'minimises' your mental struggles

Now this makes a whole lot of sense given the way we have been socialised to believe that long-standing personal or mental health problems take a long time to fix or require difficult solutions. Sometimes they do, sometimes they don't.

As you read this book, if you are suffering from a mental illness, consider also getting professional help for personalised assistance with your challenges.

Now, if you have spent the last five years being depressed, for example, you may feel embarrassed and scared to show people that you found a way to heal yourself within months, without drugs. You may fear that people will judge you. Heck, *you* might judge you. You may also feel angry at yourself for having wasted your life.

You may feel a number of negative emotions about this but just remember that if your outlook has been impaired by poor advice from well-intentioned professionals, the negative emotions you'll have experienced will have impaired your problem-solving brain. Remember how we spoke earlier of the way a whole industry has benefited from teaching people that seemingly complicated, long-standing problems require complicated, lengthy solutions? There is actually more than one industry that has benefited from this outlook, whether intentional or not. Maybe you've been the victim of one of these industries and maybe you are only now discovering that modern research and common sense clearly demonstrate a new, quick way of dealing with life's challenges, mental health, physical health, confidence, self-esteem, skills-learning, relationships and more.

So don't beat yourself up, forgive their ignorance ('for they know not what they do'), embrace what you are learning now, use it, and confidently achieve what you want to achieve. Time is something we never get back, so let's use the time we have left to our advantage.

Why Some Don't Have the Right Attitude to Trigger Resilience

The right attitude is, as Resilience Pillar 1 suggests, that life's challenges are necessary for personal growth and achievement, and so are to be welcomed. However, there are some reasons you may not posses this necessary attitude for resilience. For example:

◊ Others have always done things for you so you have not had to develop the right attitude, e.g. you have had parents and then partners who have taken all your challenges on for you.

◊ You've had a pretty happy-go-lucky life and so have not had many challenges.

◊ You have somehow come to associate problems with negative experiences only, rather than positive ones as well, e.g. you have not achieved some important goals, despite trying, and now believe problems always equate to misery.

Our repeat experiences can shape our perception and attitudes but our experiences are also shaped by our perception and attitudes. Very often, it is our perception and attitudes that lead to the reality rather than the other way around.

Let's explore this topic of attitude further because regardless of whether you fall into one of the above categories in this chapter or not, the only thing that truly matters is what you do from this point on in order to develop and maintain a habit of resilience. So without further ado, let us embrace the easy, effective strategies that are going to create the resilient you. It's about to get exciting!

Part 2:

Resilience- Strengthening

Self-Assessment Tool

*'Self-awareness is value-free. It isn't scary. It doesn't
imply that you will subject yourself to needless pain.'*
Deepak Chopra

The upcoming chapters are divided into subject categories. Within each subject category are numerous strategies that build, strengthen and maintain your resilience. Some are quick fixes for when you need them; others are easy, pleasant habits you'll maintain.

The chapter subjects will make navigation easier whenever you feel as if you need a refresh, e.g. 'I'm feeling a bit negative – I'll reread the chapters on thoughts and emotions'; 'I'm feeling unable to solve this problem, – I'll reread the chapter on problem-solving'; 'I'm feeling a little sorry for myself – I'll read the chapter on thoughts and self-care.' Keep in mind that some strategies will influence more than one Resilience Pillar at a time because everything you think, feel and do has a ripple effect.

Resilience can feel like armour off which challenges bounce rather than winding us or completely knocking us over. It's important to be able to check our resilience level, or how strong our armour is, at any given time because it helps us to make great decisions, achieve goals and maintain mental well-being. It helps us to know things like when to say 'yes' to more work and when to say 'no' to someone expecting too much of us.

Using Your Body as your Resilience-o-meter

You can easily check the current strength of your resilience
armour, or your current resilience level, at any given moment by
using the physical sensations you feel within your body. Our
bodily sensations are connected with our thoughts and emotions
and energy levels, amongst other things, as we will explore in
more detail in upcoming chapters. So you can use your bodily
sensations to:

◊ know how resilient you're feeling;
◊ work out the effects your thoughts have on your emotions;
◊ understand the effects your emotions have on your life;
◊ learn about yourself;
◊ learn about other people;
◊ learn how you feel about situations you encounter;
◊ and figure out the answers to help you solve life's many
    puzzles.

In other words, your bodily sensations can help you to learn
important answers and make great decisions. It's as though our
bodily sensations have voices if we tune in to what they have to
say. There is a huge amount of work going on inside the body at
all times and there are constant changes, some of which we can
detect, like heartbeat changes and muscles tightening or relaxing.
To use your body as a source of information, tune in to it.

   If you first need help tuning in, close your eyes and take three
or more deep breaths. As you breathe in, hold your breath for four
to five seconds and then breathe out with force.

   Now turn your mental attention away from your breathing or
the outer world and inwards to your body's inner world. Focus
your mind deep inside your body, where all the blood, water,
muscles and organs move or twitch. Simply tune in to your bodily
sensations and then listen to what they are telling you.

You might find it helps to ask yourself questions at the same time and just listen for the instinctive answers that come back, like:

◊ Where do I feel tension?
◊ What emotion does this tension relate to: anxiety, fear, sadness, pessimism . . . ?
◊ What could the reason be for me feeling this inner tension?
◊ If I'm not sure, what *might* the source of tension be?
◊ How resilient am I feeling right now?
◊ What would help me to feel more / completely resilient?

Alternatively, you can just **check how OFF you feel**:

◊ The more your bodily sensations convey **O**verwhelm, **F**atigue or **F**ragility, the more eroded your resilience armour is.
◊ The less your bodily sensations convey overwhelm, fatigue or fragility, and instead convey lightness, energy and inner strength, the more reinforced your resilience armour is.

Use this OFF acronym when you want to take a quick reading using your body as a resilience thermometer, or 'resilience-o-meter', be it in a busy restaurant, on a crowded train or with colleagues waiting for your decision. The more OFF you feel (overwhelmed, fatigued or fragile) the more eroded your resilience is. When the reading is low, simply take stock of your life, and see what's missing; the chapter titles in this book will jog your memory on where the holes in the armour may come from.

Still using your body as a resilience-o-meter, you can then pinpoint where your resilience level is up to in any given moment, much like the mercury in an actual thermometer, with the top of your head representing 100 per cent resilience and the soles of your feet representing 0 per cent. Right now, with one palm facing down, fingers pointing towards the side of the body and thumb horizontally parallel with your body, pinpoint where your resilience is. If it is feeling really eroded you might pinpoint your hip; if you're feeling really resilient right now you might determine it is around the forehead or higher.

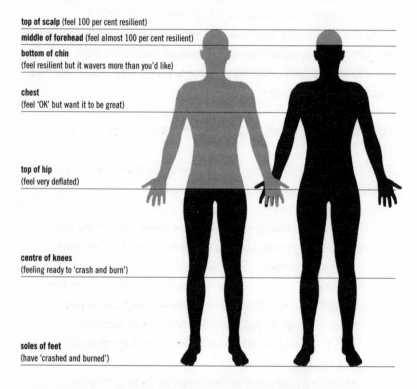

top of scalp (feel 100 per cent resilient)

middle of forehead (feel almost 100 per cent resilient)

bottom of chin
(feel resilient but it wavers more than you'd like)

chest
(feel 'OK' but want it to be great)

top of hip
(feel very deflated)

centre of knees
(feeling ready to 'crash and burn')

soles of feet
(have 'crashed and burned')

Use as required: you can now take a resilience-o-meter reading whenever you need to check if your resilience needs reinforcing, whenever someone asks to add to your workload, whenever you want to pursue a new goal or hobby, whenever something unexpected happens and you need your fighting strength, whenever . . . Practise exploring inwards before answering outwards and you will make much better decisions, enhance your self-image and resilience, and feel happier and more relaxed day-to-day.

During your four-week resilience plan: take a resilience-o-meter reading at the end of every day and note down the day, date and time to (a) see how your resilience is growing and (b) allow you to identify reasons for any dips in your readings. Nightly readings will also make you mindful of what you need to tweak from that moment on, with help from the upcoming strategies, in order to consistently maintain a high resilience reading.

As the days go by you will find your resilience reading rise, so be sure to note your readings down as they will help you to identify any patterns, like which people erode your resilience and which activities strengthen it.

⊨ OVER TO YOU ⊨

Take your first resilience reading now; you may not be able to complete step three until you've read further:

1. **TUNE IN** to what your bodily sensations are telling you about your current level of resilience. Use OFF to help (Overwhelm, Fatigue, Fragility).
2. **PINPOINT** where on your resilience-o-meter the current reading is using a body part (either of those highlighted in the diagram on page 44 or anywhere in between).
   - Is it around your hip because you're feeling really quite deflated?
   - Is it by your knee because you're feeling ready to 'crash and burn'?
   - Is it by your feet because you have 'crashed and burned'?
   - Or is it around your chest because you're 'OK' but fed up of being 'OK' and not completely happy? Or 'OK' but with frequent yo-yo-ing feelings of **O**verwhelm, **F**atigue or **F**ragility coupled with bouts of pessimism or self-doubt?

3. **PROBLEM-SOLVE** what needs to happen in order for you to get a higher resilience reading.

Finish the sentence: 'My current resilience-o-meter reading is by my . . .' Make a written note of it with a date and time.

Now all you have to do, like my coaching clients, is become a serious student of your life. Read, reflect and introspect, and carry out the simple activities described in this book, all the while checking in with your body for answers. As you do, you will notice your resilience-o-meter reading rise. If you don't, your resilience-o-meter will tell you that you need to start over from the beginning of this book. What you are about to do is simple yet powerful. That's why it works. Anyone can do it. All you have to do is tweak things here and there, and do them consistently. That. Is. It. Exciting! Let's do this!

Mind Your Attitude

'Your attitude, not your aptitude, will determine your altitude.'
Zig Ziglar

The first thing that will shape your resilient future is Resilience Pillar 1, a positive outlook on challenges. Whether we call it a positive outlook, mindset or viewpoint, **Resilience Pillar 1 is our attitude; it's the filter through which we see challenges**. That's the importance of Resilience Pillar 1 – a positive outlook on challenges – because that filter changes everything. It changes the emotions you experience, the decisions you make, the way that you behave, and the thoughts you have about people, places, events, objects and yourself.

Sometimes you don't even realise you've been holding a negative mindset, all the while accidentally sabotaging yourself at every turn with your skewed negative outlook, lack of self-belief and disproportionate focus on the problems instead of the solutions. Sometimes, you can have a positive attitude in most areas of your life but a negative attitude towards a particular challenge you've been facing for some time.

Here's the thing: I have plenty of intelligent clients – I mean really intelligent, really successful-in-their-careers clients – who don't even realise their outlook has been sabotaging them in the area they want my help with. For whatever reason, and this may resonate with you, some of them have honed a self-serving positive attitude towards certain challenges whilst having a self-sabotaging negative attitude towards challenges in other areas or one other area. For example, they may use every challenge to their advantage in the workplace but become completely bewildered when facing challenges in their dating life. Or they may be the sage of their social group but when they struggle to change careers they become completely unnerved.

If we hold the self-serving positive attitude that life's challenges are events and lessons that guide us towards our goals, happiness and life purpose, then we ask ourselves questions like:

◊ What is this trying to teach me?
◊ What do I need to achieve in order to overcome this challenge?
◊ Where can I get the necessary information from?
◊ Who can help me?

If you hold the self-sabotaging negative attitude that life's challenges are unfortunate events that block us from our goals, happiness and life purpose, then we ask ourselves questions like:

◊ Why is this happening to me?
◊ Why do I never seem to be able to achieve this goal?
◊ Will I ever achieve this goal?
◊ Am I just unworthy of good fortune?

To face challenges with resilience you need a self-serving, positive outlook (Resilience Pillar 1) so let's check where yours is right now, and don't worry about the answer.

⊨ OVER TO YOU ⊨

A) If you feel you have one overall outlook on challenges, finish this sentence: 'My outlook on life's challenges is that . . .' Or, if you feel that you have varied outlooks for different areas of your life, finish this sentence for each: 'My outlook on the challenges in this area is that . . .'

Areas to consider: (a) family, (b) love life, (c) work/career, (d) money/income, (e) power and status, (f) health/fitness/appearance, (g) spirituality, (h) contribution to others, (i) leisure/fun, (j) friends and social life.

As this is an entirely private exercise, be completely honest with yourself. Remember, no critical judgements; as you come on this journey with me you're just being a great student of your life and self.

B) Next, identify whether your current attitude(s) are closer to the self-sabotaging negative end where Resilience Pillar 1 is absent or closer to the opposite, self-serving positive end of the spectrum where Resilience Pillar 1 sits.

Self-Sabotaging: Life's challenges are unfortunate events that block us from our goals, happiness and life purpose.		**Self-Serving:** Life's challenges are events and lessons that guide us towards our goals, happiness and life purpose.

Identify which areas of your life you need to work on and pick one to work on first (the one that feels the most important to work on right now). Then, as you make progress, you can start working on the other areas, as you feel ready to.

⊢⸺⊣

Move Along, Move Along, Nothing (Worthwhile) to See Here

Resilience requires that we have a positive outlook on challenges (Resilience Pillar 1) and, as we saw on pages 24–5, positive thoughts result in positive emotions whilst negative thoughts result in negative emotions and can initiate the fight-or-flight response within us. Negative emotions also disrupt our brain's cognitive functions[3] – things like critical thinking, working memory and decision-making. Therefore, if we want to resiliently overcome life's challenges, we need our critical-thinking, problem-solving brain functions working to their optimum level.

Choosing a positive outlook or attitude (Resilience Pillar 1) leads to positive emotions which help your brain work as it's meant to, enabling you to problem-solve skilfully (Resilience Pillar 3) and overcome challenges resiliently!

However close to the self-sabotaging end of the spectrum your attitude is right now, it is as temporary or fixed as you choose it to be. Just like the school children who improved their mathematics grades, you can change your fate by adjusting your attitude. We humans change our attitudes all the time when it suits us, and we can do it in a split second.

Maya Angelou famously said, 'If you don't like something, change it. If you can't change it, change your attitude.' We've all been there – suddenly found ourselves changing our attitude within seconds, all for justified reasons, of course . . . For example, Dawn wants to stay in one evening because she's feeling tired and the wet weather isn't motivating her. She genuinely believes, 'I think I need to rest and recuperate this weekend,' and tells her friend this. Dawn's friend keeps insisting that Dawn 'come out' and then mentions that Dawn's big romantic crush is going to be out as well. Suddenly, motivated by the idea of seeing the object of her affections, Dawn has a change of attitude towards going out with her friend: *I can wear my new top,* she thinks to herself, *and if I stay home all weekend I won't feel as if I've achieved much, so I think going out will be good for me.* Then she tells her friend so, much to her friend's contentment. We've all had those fast turnaround moments and in this type of situation it was because Dawn was **motivated to change her attitude or perspective**.

⊨ **OVER TO YOU** ⊨

Think of a recent time when you rapidly changed your attitude:

- What was the original attitude?
- What was the new attitude?
- What positive outcomes did you achieve as a result of that quick change of attitude?

This could be something big like, you wanted to have children, discovered you couldn't and so changed your attitude to focus on why it's so great being child-free. This type of sudden attitude change helps save us from a great deal of heartache. Or it could be something small like changing your attitude towards tennis from negative to positive because you fell in love with someone who loves tennis, and changing your attitude helped you to bond.

⊨⊨

Sometimes we change our attitude because the direction of our motivation suddenly changes, as we saw with Dawn. Other times we change our attitude because we want to ease emotional pain or avoid it outright, e.g. 'It's probably just as well that I failed the test because I'm not sure I want to pursue that career anyway.' Other times we change our attitude because we want to avoid conflict or think it will help us to maintain a positive relationship with someone, e.g. 'It's OK that my partner hasn't paid any attention to me for a few months because he's under a lot of pressure at the moment.'

Notice how when the goal is one we're motivated to achieve (Resilience Pillar 2), we automatically become motivated to change our attitude or outlook (Resilience Pillar 1); we can do it within moments and this can be a good thing – a self-serving mechanism that helps us to survive, maintain our mental well-being and achieve our goals. However, we can also change our attitude to avoid immediate problems or pain, and by doing so, accidentally create long-term problems and pain and miss goals instead! Then it can be a self-sabotaging mechanism.

Using the examples above: What if you need to take a retest because that career *is* what you want to do and you are only trying to convince yourself otherwise because you are trying to avoid immediate feelings of failure and the chore of having to do more studying? What if your avoidance of conflict around your partner's recent inattentiveness actually leads to a bigger distance between you, and more problems?

Be very clear that you are adopting an attitude that comes from a place aimed at achieving the goals you believe are important to your overall health and happiness in the long-run, rather than acting out of avoidance or fear in the short-run. Rest assured, as we go through the book, you will make this choice easily because you'll notice that:

A. emotional pain is much more our friend than our enemy: it signposts us towards health and happiness by telling us that something doesn't feel good and needs fixing (emotions are a source of knowledge);

B. whatever we focus on, we work towards: whether that is our fears or our goals.

Being able to change our attitude within moments is a very good thing and vital for reinforcing our resilience armour, so long as we do so based on goals, not fear or pain avoidance. Always pursue goals based on long-term, long-lasting health and happiness even if it means encountering short-term, short-lived pain or inconvenience.

Changing Our Attitude Helps us to Learn, Grow and Achieve

One simple and effective way to change our attitude towards challenges or negative situations is to shift our perspective.

I remember the case of Daniel D, a successful business executive. Daniel's upbringing was one he hadn't remembered fondly; specifically, he recalled how disconnected he had felt from his father his entire childhood and even now. He felt strongly that his father hadn't ever really cared about him but the more we explored his home dynamics during childhood, the more I saw a father who perhaps loved his son but was seemingly inept at demonstrating it. As we spoke of these insights, Daniel started to tweak his perspective on his father and his eyes lit up. Maybe he had misunderstood his father.

I asked Daniel to consider starting anew in getting to know who his father was . . . for the first time in his life. You see, Daniel had viewed his father his whole life through the eyes of that hurt child who felt uncared for or even unloved. I suggested he get acquainted with his father, instead, through the eyes of an adult who was merely meeting a near-stranger and trying to get to know him. The goal was to suspend all preconceived ideas of his father that stemmed from the experiences and perspectives of the young Daniel, which may have been a complete misunderstanding. Unless, as adults, we explore a person's character, their thought-processes, their motivations and their attitudes, we can hold on to the skewed evaluations we made of them as hurt children.

A simple tweak in perspective meant a world of difference to Daniel's resilience and you could see it unfold right there and then in that moment in the session. Daniel and I spoke about his father's interests and hobbies and Daniel decided that instead of only apprehensively seeing his father to 'check in on him', he would take him out to do something fun. This would give Daniel and his father the opportunity to connect as adults. Truly, for the first time in his life, he was going to try to get to know his father, and he seemed excited. Wow! Within that first coaching session we went from him being a hurt, almost 'emotionless' man to an optimistic, excited man making plans to spend quality time with the father he barely knew how to relate to.

Importantly, a shift in **perspective** meant that Daniel was able to change his attitude, experience a different set of **emotions** for his father after all those years, and subsequently employ a different set of **behaviours** to help improve their relationship. More on the ripple effect of a change in perspective later on.

How Our Attitudes Affect us without us Realising It

Sometimes the filters look like reality until we notice and question them. Attitudes are powerful; they can make us blind or acutely aware, happy or sad, optimistic or pessimistic, compassionate or contemptuous – the list goes on.

You might notice other people's attitudes (filters) more than your own as you hear those struggling to achieve an important goal of theirs make negative, judgemental statements about their challenges, and see them indulge self-sabotaging behaviours.

Our attitudes affect our judgements and behaviours in two distinct ways: 'spontaneously' and 'deliberatively'.[4]

The **spontaneous process** is when our attitudes guide our behaviour without us consciously thinking about how our attitudes are influencing us. We see this clearly in people who are prejudiced against a certain racial group, for example; these people can be prejudiced towards a person without recognising that they are perceiving or behaving in a way that is influenced by their prejudices. In this process, our brain automatically activates an attitude's filter, colouring how we perceive that person or object.

Automatically activated attitudes first shape our perceptions, and then our judgements and behaviours. So, without us being consciously aware of it, our behaviour towards a person or object can be influenced by the attitudes we already hold towards them.

The **deliberative process** is when we consciously evaluate (deliberate) the costs and benefits of pursuing one course of action over another, which means we consider our attitudes (our filters) whilst deciding on a plan of action. As this process requires effort, whilst the 'spontaneous' one does not, research suggests we have to be motivated to expend the mental effort and have the time and resources, like money, to follow it.

So your attitudes are shaping your behaviour and yet you may not even be aware of how.

⊨ OVER TO YOU ⊨

Thinking of the goals that seem to be out of your reach, what are the 'spontaneous' or 'automatic' attitudes you have about the challenges in the way of those goals? Write from the heart without overthinking your answers. Finish these sentences:

- 'The automatic attitudes I have about the challenges in the way of my important goals are . . .' (For example: men only ever want me for one thing.)
- 'These automatic attitudes could be sabotaging my goals by influencing me to behave in the following ways . . .'
- 'When I change my attitude to viewing these challenges as opportunities for learning and growth, I have learnt the following valuable lessons that will ultimately help me to achieve my goals . . .'

When you have automatic attitudes about challenges, you've stopped checking if they stem from your frustrations or objective reality. If they reflect your frustrations but you don't question them, you'll block yourself from possible solutions to your problems and you'll create more issues than already existed. This is the ripple effect of your thoughts – the power of thoughts – which we'll explore in more detail in the next chapter.

Remember: use every challenge as an opportunity to learn and benefit. This sometimes requires (a) exploring your automatic attitudes that at one time were not automatic, and then (b) actively changing your attitudes to become better aligned with your goals. This may take a bit of effort at first, but soon these more positive attitudes will come automatically. Healthy people learn how to adjust their thoughts frequently to make reality comfortable and reasonable.

⊨―――⊏

Interestingly, other motivations also play a role in how much our attitudes affect our response to a person or object. Sometimes we want to believe in something so much that we will pretend we believe that our dreams are our reality. For example, research on romantic relationships found that when the person believed they had invested considerably in their relationship and had few relationship alternatives, they were more motivated to view their relationship favourably. As a result, these people would over-report relationship positivity to repress their true relationship doubts because they did not want to end the relationship or felt they couldn't.[5]

Our attitudes are guiding our behaviours all the time – sometimes consciously, other times subconsciously. How much we consciously think about our attitudes depends on whether we are motivated to and have the resources to (e.g. time, money and energy to access our memory). This suggests that **when we are highly motivated to achieve an end goal (Resilience Pillar 2) we pay greater attention to whether we have a positive outlook on challenges (Resilience Pillar 1)**, and when we do, we employ a problem-solving approach (Resilience Pillar 3).

So, given you have picked up this book and have chosen to

come on this journey with me, make the choice to carry a self-serving positive attitude as you study your life and self.

Whilst your attitude is the filter through which you view people and things, as Resilience Pillar 1 is the filter through which we view challenges, in the next chapter we'll look at thoughts in more detail, showing you how to steer your life in the direction you want to go in.

SUMMARY

Your attitude is shaping how you're dealing with your challenges right now, and we've learnt that you can change your attitude whenever you want, in an instant.

The power of changing your attitude is that it will reveal insights to you that you had previously shut your mind off from, possibly for years.

If you want those insights that will get your life and happiness on track, embrace Resilience Pillar 1 – a positive outlook on challenges – as your attitude towards challenges from this moment on. As we have seen, all it requires is that you are motivated to review your current attitude on challenges and are prepared to move it towards Resilience Pillar 1 if necessary.

The Power of Thinking

'We are disturbed not by what happens to us, but by our thoughts about what happens to us.' Epictetus

What a great statement: so true. It's not what happens but how we evaluate what happens that shapes its impact upon us, our lives, our loved ones and mankind itself.

You already know that two people can witness the exact same thing and have a completely different view of it. In fact, we feel deeply connected with the people who frequently perceive things in the same way we do. We usually call them our closest family and friends for that very reason.

That power of connection between two people who have perceived an event, person or situation in the same way highlights how much we know that thoughts are subjective meanings we attach to events, even if we don't actively think about it. In fact, we are so used to *not* thinking about it that we can believe we have no choice over how we think. That's a nail in your resilience coffin right there, so pull it out if you've hammered it in and let's think about thinking for a moment, whilst you hold onto that nail.

Thoughts shape things and they make things happen. If you want to change your life, you must improve your thinking and how you speak to others. Your words are steering your life; they are your hands on the steering wheel of your life, moving it left, moving it right, driving straight, driving smoothly, making jerky manoeuvres, and maybe honking your horn along the way.

⊨ OVER TO YOU ⊨

Roughly speaking, (a) what percentage of your minute-to-minute thoughts are positive versus negative, and (b) how would you rate your mental well-being? Complete these sentences in written or typed form:

- 'My minute-to-minute thoughts are __ per cent positive and __ per cent negative.'
- 'My mental well-being minute-to-minute is . . .'

Putting aside the reason for the percentage split, as you look at the answers you have given, what connection do you see between the percentage of positive versus negative thoughts, and your mental well-being?

Don't worry if you score really high on the negativity scale – it is something that you will change because you want to become resilient. As negative thoughts are at the root of many problems, it is important to take stock of your overriding thoughts whenever your resilience wavers.

⊨⊨

In coaching I use an alternative version of Cognitive Behavioural Therapy's Hot Cross Bun (5 Areas) Model called the Thought–Feedback Cycle (see diagrams overleaf). Both models help you to see exactly how your thoughts, attitudes and outlooks affect your life and how you can choose positive thoughts to produce positive outcomes.

Hot Cross Bun Model (CBT)

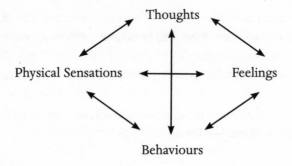

Thought–Feedback Cycle

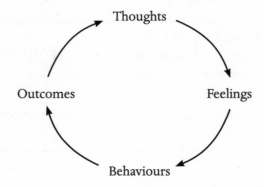

When you choose a frequently recurring negative thought and take it through the cycle, listing the resulting emotions, behaviours, outcomes and subsequent thoughts, you'll notice a **pattern of self-sabotage**. When you then run through the exercise again, this time replacing the negative thought with a realistic positive one, you'll notice a **self-serving pattern** emerge. The only difference? The thoughts you choose to attach to situations, events and people.

By making better choices about the thoughts you use, you take better control of your emotions and behaviours, ushering yourself in the direction of your goals.

Imagine for a moment that Rita holds the thought (outlook) that she is unlikely to find her Mr Right to spend her life with versus the thought (outlook) that she is absolutely going to find her Mr Right to spend her life with:

Thoughts/Outlook:	Rita holds the thought (outlook) that she is **unlikely to** find her Mr Right	Rita holds the thought (outlook) that she is **absolutely going to** find her Mr Right
Behaviours: How many hours might Rita spend proactively searching for Mr Right?	*An hour or so a month, or just minutes each month*	*Several hours a week or several hours a month*
Emotions: How might Rita react if asked on a date by a seemingly nice, genuine person?	*Cynicism and/or anxiety*	*Excitement and/or optimism*
Outcomes: How likely is it that Rita still won't have found her Mr Right three years from now?	*Likely or highly likely*	*Unlikely or highly unlikely*

Over-simplified? Yes, but you get the gist. The example illustrates the effect our thoughts have on our emotions and behaviours and, thus, the outcomes we achieve in life.

⊨ OVER TO YOU ⊨

Put your thoughts into the Thought–Feedback Cycle. It will take you about thirty seconds to go through the cycle. Finish these sentences:

a. 'A frequently recurring negative thought I have is . . .'
b. 'The emotions I experience as a result of that negative thought are . . .'
c. 'The behaviours I indulge as a result of those negative emotions are . . .'
d. 'The outcomes I achieve as a result of such behaviours are . . .'
e. 'The subsequent thoughts I have that feed back into my emotions as the cycle continues are . . .'

Notice the pattern of self-sabotage? Next, repeat this exercise by starting with a positive, alternative thought you could have about the same topic. Notice the more self-serving pattern that emerges?

Recognising the enormity of this thoughts–outcomes link gives you the power to stop your thoughts before they hamper your mood, screw up your decisions and actions, and push your goals further away. Instead, you practise using positive thoughts, even if it feels a little fake and silly at first, because positive thoughts are the starting point of achieving anything, as will become clear throughout this book.

Who has the most control over our thoughts? We do. If we make a conscious effort to choose positive thoughts, we generate positive feelings, which tend to result in 'positive behaviours' that will help us to achieve our goals – positive outcomes.

Whatever you say to yourself, silently or aloud, tells your brain what to focus on. Simple! What are you telling your brain to focus on in each moment? How difficult things are or how easy things are, how fortunate you are or how unfortunate you are, how much others control your life or how much you are in control of your life? Take control of your thoughts and you take control of your life.

Choose the Right Feedback Loop

When we allow ourselves to dwell on negative thoughts we are much more likely to feel unhappy, powerless and pessimistic. However, when we consciously choose to focus on positive thoughts, we create what I refer to as a 'positive feedback loop' (somewhat different from the definition in science) and, therefore, we are much more likely to feel happy, in control and optimistic.

Interestingly, what is similar between the definition of positive and negative feedback loops in science and in the context of your Thought–Feedback Cycle is that:

◊ positive feedback loops in science are defined as **enhancing and amplifying changes**, whilst
◊ negative feedback loops in science are defined as **dampening or buffering changes**.

Our thoughts work a lot like that. Positive thoughts enhance our lives and negative thoughts dampen our lives. One might also say that positive thoughts make our experience of life more pleasurable whilst negative thoughts cushion us from fully enjoying positive life experiences or skew our perception of life towards the negative.

If we've habitually been in a problem-focused mindset ('negative feedback loop'), we will find that our thinking, when left on 'auto-pilot', tends to be negative. Consciously thinking about things more positively initially takes more conscious effort than subconscious negative thinking. However, the more we practise facing challenges with a positive outlook (Resilience Pillar 1) and a focus on solutions (Resilience Pillar 3), the more we mould our ever-evolving brain to immediately face challenges with resilience. So if you have a habit of thinking negatively, the goal is to go from subconscious negative thinking to subconscious positive thinking by transitioning from stage one to stage four:

1. **Subconscious negative thinking habit** (have a habit of automatically thinking negatively most of the time without realising it)
2. **Conscious negative thinking** (have a habit of thinking negatively most of the time but are now aware of it)
3. **Conscious positive thinking** (actively creating a habit of thinking positively most of the time with conscious effort)
4. **Subconscious positive thinking habit** (have a habit of automatically thinking positively most of the time without trying to)

Let's look at why it's important to our mental well-being, goals and resilience that we choose our thoughts wisely.

Mindfulness Meditation Changes the Brain's Structure

Mindfulness is being present: focusing only on what we're absorbing through our senses, right here, right now, in this moment. When I have anxious or depressed clients who use mindfulness or mindfulness mediation, they transform their inner peace. They begin to feel empowered because rather than feeling at the mercy of their mind, their brain and their thoughts, they feel in control of their mind and their once self-sabotaging thoughts. They have found a way out of the inner chaos and have replaced it with inner stillness regardless of what else is going on 'out there'. When you focus on living in the present, you will experience a feeling of euphoria. Doing so also highlights how our thoughts can sabotage not only our goals, but also our inner peace; regardless of what else is going on in the outside world, it's your inner world that is always shaping your outer world . . . or your life.

Try it! The next time you are making a cup of tea, or eating a biscuit, or driving somewhere, or sitting on a sofa, get out of your mind and into the present moment by focusing only on what you can see, hear, feel, smell and taste. Your worries and stresses will slip away and relaxation and peace will take over, even if just for those few moments.

It's not just a temporary state, though. How we use our brain most frequently remoulds its structure and how it works. This is why you'll no longer use your brain in the sort of slapdash manner you might have used until now!

To give you an inside look at what your thoughts do to your brain: in one study, meditation novices were asked to use a basic mindfulness meditation practice for eight weeks. After eight weeks, the participants' brains had physically changed. Compared with their own pre-meditation brain scans and the participants who didn't meditate, the meditating participants had increased the concentration of (the amount of grey matter in) the parts of the brain involved in learning, memory, emotion-regulation, perspective- taking, and processing information in relation to ourselves.[6]

What's more, in a previous study led by the same leading researcher, a positive correlation was discovered between a reduction in stress and a decrease in grey matter density in the amygdala, the brain region that plays an important role in stress and anxiety.[7]

Therefore, not thinking negative thoughts is good for your brain and frequent negative thoughts are bad for your brain, as they train your brain to become really good at being anxious and stressed. In fact, a frequent release of stress hormones can damage the emotion-regulation centres of your brain,[8] making it more difficult to manage emotions than it is for someone who mostly thinks positive thoughts. Indulging negative thoughts all the time is as bad for your mental health as eating junk food every day is for your physical health. It's easier for us to be aware of what we're putting into our mouth and body than into our mind and brain, because food is visible and thoughts aren't. This is why we have to think about the nature of our thoughts, especially regarding the stuff we think about frequently. Clearly, it is up to us to restructure our brain with care.

⊨ OVER TO YOU ⊨

If you have a tendency to worry all the time or a lot of the time, then get serious about retraining your brain with a simple mindfulness meditation exercise. You can use a mini-version of this day-to-day, too.

The 'long meditation':

- Sit or lie somewhere warm and relaxing.
- Set an alarm for ten to thirty minutes and close your eyes.
- Take three to seven deep breaths, inhaling slowly, holding for a few seconds and then exhaling slowly.
- Mentally scan your body for any tense muscles and relax each one by just letting go.
- For the remaining time simply focus your mind on your breathing.
- Each time a thought pops into your mind, observe it without analysis or judgement, imagine it floating away with the clouds or getting washed away in a river, and then refocus on your breathing.

The 'mini meditation' is the same as above but you can:

- Set the alarm for one to five minutes.
- Use the breathing exercise to relax: inhale slowly, hold your breath for a few seconds and exhale slowly (three to seven times).
- Sit, lie or stand for the meditation.

These practices calm the mind and help generate inner peace as we learn how to live in the moment: not in our heads, not in the past and not thinking about something in the future; just right here in the present moment, just being.

Do the meditations as often as you can and work them into your lifestyle. If you find mini-meditations effective and more achievable, do them daily as and when you can and when you feel you need help relaxing. If you need to make more drastic changes to your mental well-being because of how you've been moulding your brain for a while, do the long meditations three to seven times a week. Remember, the more you train it, the more you will change it.

Now we know that our mere thoughts and habits can change our brain's size, structure and function, let's look at how we can break bad habits and replace them with good habits to achieve resilience.

Habits in the Brain

The brain creates new habits with **focus**, **consistency** and **repetition**.[9] Once strongly reinforced, habits can become automatic so that an event triggers the automated response without the person consciously thinking about what they're doing, and consequently an outcome is achieved, whether desirable or not. Think of a smoker who just has to smoke after a meal, even if he had a cigarette half an hour earlier and usually only smokes once every hour. Or the person who has to drink a glass of wine every evening by around 8 p.m. to unwind. These people weren't born with these requirements – heck, they may not have even done this a year ago – but now such behaviours have become a must because they've wired their brain to expect that one must coincide with the other. This is how addictions are created and take over a person's life, but it's also how we create our simple daily habits, good or bad; whether brushing our teeth, arguing with our spouse or crumbling at every challenge obstructing our goal. Something will trigger the response as if by automatic reflex, e.g. the fact that we've just washed our face first thing in the morning, or our spouse just started a sentence with, 'Why are the kids still—?' or a customer is getting upset on the phone.

Habits can be hypnotising. Once habits are created, we often stop consciously thinking about whether their outcomes are moving us towards our goals or away from them. We just let the brain make decisions based on what we've done in the past. These 'automated' habits allow the brain to work efficiently with minimal effort, conserving our energy for other tasks like learning a new skill. This is the brain working efficiently as far as it is concerned but it's unhelpful when the brain's been trained into bad habits.

Retrain Your Brain

So how does the brain actually create habits that can become automatic behaviours we carry out over and over again? Remember Pavlov's dogs experiment from Part 1?

The brain contains individual neurons which process and transmit information through electrical and chemical signals. To accomplish even the simplest tasks, such as walking and brushing your teeth, the brain requires a large number of interconnected neurons to work together as a team to process and transmit all the necessary information.

Now, a change of habit (breaking the old habit and replacing it with a new one) requires us to make a conscious choice to change our existing neural networks by training the brain to modify them and create new ones.

There are three useful terms from the world of neuroplasticity research that you should mentally carry around with you to help you to think about how you are rewiring your brain all the time. They are: 'neurons that fire together wire together', 'neurons that fire apart wire apart', and the 'use it or lose it' brain.[9]

In simple terms, when two things repeatedly and consistently occur simultaneously or near simultaneously, the brain begins to associate one with the other. Consequently, the occurrence of one can then trigger the occurrence of the other without much thought, if any, because 'neurons that fire together wire together'. If you then want to break a habit, you must stop indulging it, forcing the neurons to consistently fire at different times and thereby breaking the brain's association of one with the other because 'neurons that fire apart wire apart'. The brain comes to treat them as separate 'events' rather than intertwined 'events' so that eventually one will no longer trigger the other as the brain will no longer expect them to occur simultaneously or near simultaneously.

The third term, the 'use it or lose it' brain, refers to how the brain 'prunes away' any neural connections that are not being used. This is why it's so important to repeatedly use skills we have honed so we don't lose them through lack of use. This is also partially why the brain declines into old age – we allow skills to degenerate through lack of use as the brain responds to how we are exercising it. Therefore, we can lose an old skill through lack of use because we either 'use it or lose it' and in the exact same way we can lose (eliminate) self-sabotaging habits to the point where we have no desire to repeat them.

Training the brain to change a habit requires a simple three-step process:

1. Identify the trigger that sparks the habitual response before the habitual response is indulged, e.g. the kids running amok at bedtime (**trigger**).
2. Consciously and consistently abandon the old response every time the trigger occurs, e.g. feeling bewildered and out of control and shouting at the kids (**habitual undesirable response**).
3. Consciously and consistently use the new response you want to reinforce every time the trigger occurs, e.g.

remembering you're in control and talking to the kids in a calm, assertive manner (**new, desirable response you want to make habitual**).

Indulge a consistent pattern for about two to three hours a day and the brain can start to make visible changes within just forty-eight hours.[10]

Changing habits is easy when you realise you just need a period of sustained effort where you **consciously change** how you're responding to a trigger or otherwise alter a pattern you've been following. Soon enough, that new response or pattern becomes the habit and you can stop thinking about it so much once the brain starts executing it fairly automatically. This is just like learning to drive a car or play a musical instrument. At first we have to really consciously think about every action but eventually we can execute the task without much thought, fairly automatically. Instead of learning how to drive or play a musical instrument, you're simply learning how to respond to all challenges with resilience until you do so without much thought . . . fairly automatically. Just like learning how to drive a car or play an instrument, the more you practise resilience each day at every opportunity, the quicker you will master resilience. You must also be as consistent as possible – face all challenges with an immediate resilient response because we have a 'use it or lose it' brain. You must teach your brain to lose the fear, panic, pessimism and self-doubt responses to challenges and instead hone the responses of calm, optimism, excitement and self-confidence, much of which stems from your outlook.

Rewire Your Brain for Resilience

To rewire your brain for resilience, you must make a conscious effort to respond to every challenge with Resilience Pillar 1, a positive outlook on the challenge, closely followed by Resilience Pillar 3, a problem-solving approach.

So that's:
1. notice challenge;
2. have an immediate positive outlook on the challenge;
3. immediately begin to problem-solve until you overcome the challenge.

Completely problem-solving the challenge may take time, and that's fine. The important point is to back up your immediate positive outlook with affirmative action straight away to reassure your brain and mind that you are indeed going to overcome the challenge. This immediate problem-solving can be as simple as thinking of possible solutions in your mind or brainstorming ideas on paper, as we will discuss in the chapter on creative problem-solving (see page 174).

The great thing is, as a positive thought, Resilience Pillar 1 (a positive outlook on challenges) naturally results in positive emotions like optimism and self-belief, and these naturally elevate our motivation (Resilience Pillar 2) and naturally propel us to problem-solve (Resilience Pillar 3). In other words, Resilience Pillar 1 automatically strengthens Resilience Pillars 2 and 3, as a welcome side-effect.

Think about how your brain is being wired when you have a negative self-sabotaging outlook on challenges, i.e. when Resilience Pillar 1 is absent. If every time you faced a challenge you always indulged 'negative feedback loops', you'd be wiring together your awareness of challenges with negative self-sabotaging thoughts, negative self-sabotaging emotions (like powerlessness, sadness, insecurity and anxiety) and negative self-sabotaging and goal-sabotaging behaviours like incorrect actions or inaction. That's how non-resilient people wire their brains. You are not going to do that (any more). You are going to take the easy, smart route to resilience:

1. **Notice challenge**
2. **Have an immediate positive outlook**
3. **Problem-solve**

Our thoughts shape our life. Always remember that. Everything you currently do or don't do when it comes to facing challenges resiliently ultimately stems from your thoughts. Get Resilience Pillar 1 in place (a positive outlook on challenges) and the other pillars will naturally come into being, particularly Resilience Pillar 3, a problem-solving approach, which is how you overcome the challenges.

Now that neuroscience clearly demonstrates that we ourselves are influencing the neural networks we are building in our brain, you must take charge of which neurons you want firing together and which you want firing apart.

⊨ OVER TO YOU ⊨

To rewire your brain for a resilience habit from this point on, meet every challenge you encounter (trigger) with an immediate positive outlook on challenges (Resilience Pillar 1) closely followed by a problem-solving approach (Resilience Pillar 3). Just remember:

1. **Notice challenge** (trigger)
2. **Positive outlook** (Resilience Pillar 1)
3. **Problem-solve** (Resilience Pillar 3)

For now, as we are yet to explore problem-solving strategies (Resilience Pillar 3), you can practise a problem-solving approach using your common sense.

To rewire your brain for any other habit you currently want to change, you may find it helpful to write down (a) what the triggers are and (b) how you would rather respond to those triggers in the future, in terms of better thoughts and behaviours. The triggers could be a particular person or situation, someone's behaviour, a place you visit, and so on. Then, *every time* you encounter one of your listed triggers, you must do two things:

i. break the old habit by consistently NOT using the old response;

ii. create the new habit by consciously and consistently using the new more desirable response you've listed for each trigger, at every opportunity you get.

Watching Clients Embrace Resilience

Some people believe that they are at the mercy of their thoughts and that a situation or event has triggered their thoughts. By exploring human thoughts in more detail, you come to realise that the way you evaluate and respond to a situation or event is in your control and starts with you taking charge of the way you think about the situation or event.

When Jemima C came into coaching she was struggling to gain cooperation from her children and so felt like she was underperforming as a full-time mother. She was frustrated and anxious, and she felt powerless in the situation. When we started coaching, Jemima's outlook on her challenges increasingly unnerved her: she took every challenge as a sign that she was underperforming as a mother rather than as a lesson or other benefit that was ushering her towards her goals and happiness. After a few coaching sessions Jemima eventually embraced the idea that how she was thinking, feeling and behaving was influencing her children's behaviour, rather than the children's behaviour influencing her thoughts, emotions and behaviours. Her thoughts made her feel frustrated and angry, which then affected how she communicated with the children, which meant in turn that they didn't obey her as often or as easily as she would have liked, and she then felt bad about herself. When she chose more neutral or positive thoughts about her challenge, such as 'They're just pushing boundaries as kids do' and 'I can do this' (changing how she responded to the triggers), she experienced less anxiety and frustration and more self-confidence, and this in turn meant the children cooperated more often and more easily than before, and Jemima felt better about herself, too.

Success and progress in anything come from ownership; we are the driving force behind our own life experience. We are responsible for what we achieve in life. This is why Resilience Pillar 1 – a positive outlook on challenges – is so important.

That Nail You're Holding

Do you now believe that you have a choice over how you think, and believe you must take charge of your thinking? If so, take the nail that you could've hammered into your resilience coffin and, using your mind's eye, feel it in your hand as you roll it back and forth between your fingers. Then visualise yourself throwing that nail into a bin, with pleasure. What a relief! You are no longer imprisoning yourself in the idea that someone else or something else is in control of you; you are in control of you and your life. Congratulations: you are well and truly on the journey to a resilient you. Now, let's really use the power of thoughts to our advantage.

Have a (Positive) Word with Yourself

You may have heard of positive self-talk or affirmations (positive statements) but you might not understand what they mean – or perhaps they have always felt like mumbo jumbo to you. Positive self-talk, or talking to ourselves positively, helps us to take charge of our thought–feedback loops in a positive, self-serving and mankind-serving way; it can also help us to improve our skills and achieve our goals.

Since my late teens I had listened to incredibly successful people talking about the importance of positive self-talk (talking positively to yourself). Then when I began my coaching practice some years ago, I experienced first-hand the power of positive thinking and the use of positive self-talk from my clients' self-reports. Clients would come back to me two weeks after we had agreed they would create affirmations and repeat them daily, reporting significant changes in their outlook and outcomes and in the goals they were achieving. They were upbeat, bouncy and optimistic, and better able to think and act in line with their goals. Two weeks! I was astounded. The speed with which they were becoming resilient and moving towards their goals demonstrated for me the power positive thoughts hold over our lives . . . and the power of the negative ones, too!

Remember, whatever you focus your mind on, you will consciously and subconsciously work towards. Positive self-talk ensures you have a greater volume of positive thoughts minute-to-minute, thoughts that will direct your mind's attention in the right way. Talking kindly to yourself, frequently, can bring you out of the pits of despair or defuse great frustration, and can make you feel calm, confident and happy, because it effectively alters what you focus your mind on and what you do. Talking positively to yourself can also help you achieve anything, like giving a groom's speech, teaching a class, furthering your career or business, losing weight, getting fit, doing well in an interview, learning a new skill, having better relationships with your loved ones, finishing the current task in the limited time you have . . . the list is endless.

The more you focus your mind in the direction of your goals rather than your fears or frustrations, and in the direction of optimism rather than pessimism, of self-belief rather than self-doubt, the more you will achieve and the happier you will be. It's like the difference between meandering in the direction of your goals and jogging or even galloping in that direction, whether your goal is an emotion (like happiness or calm) or a concrete achievement (like securing a business deal or losing weight for your wedding day). Good self-talk helps ensure your thought–feedback cycles – and your life – are spiralling in a positive direction rather than a negative one.

A growing body of research tells us why we should be using self-talk for better emotions and achieving goals.

Sport is a great place to test the effects of how we talk to ourselves because we can do it in a measured way. One analysis of thirty-two sports psychology studies that, combined, measured sixty-two effects of self-talk, revealed that self-talk does indeed improve sport performance.[11] **'Instructional' self-talk** appears to be consistently more effective for precision-oriented tasks like fine motor skills (e.g. 'arm straight') and hand–eye co-ordination tasks like dart-throwing. **'Motivational' self-talk** seems to be better for improving our overall confidence and self-belief that we are capable of acting in accordance with, and achieving, our goals (e.g. 'I am capable' or 'I feel good').[12]

So you could say one type of self-talk improves our behaviours and the other type improves our emotions. For example, to help you deliver a great presentation to a room of peers, you might use the instructional self-talk 'Breathe calmly' and 'Make good eye contact throughout' coupled with motivational self-talk: 'I feel confident' and 'I enjoy teaching this topic'. The result would be a better presentation and a more enjoyable experience for you.

Elsewhere, in a large-scale study of over 44,000 people playing an online game, self-talk focused on improving results (e.g. 'I can beat my best score') as well as on the methods employed (e.g. 'I can react quicker this time'). Both improved the gamers' achievements.[13] So in this case the self-talk was focused on what they were going to achieve (end goal) and how (behaviours).

So positive self-talk moves us in the direction of our goals when it is focused on desired:

◊ emotions;
◊ behaviours;
◊ outcomes/goals.

The analysis of the thirty-two sports psychology studies also revealed that the more specific the instructional self-talk is the more effective it is. That makes sense. Words tell us what to focus on, whether we're listening to how we're talking to ourselves or listening to someone else talking to us.

You already intuitively know that it would unnerve you if someone stood criticising you and your abilities just before you had to perform an important task, and you also know that words of encouragement can be powerful. The same goes for achieving something important that requires a long-term focus and ongoing effort. So all we're really talking about is applying that same common sense to how we talk to ourselves. Research even demonstrates that the language centres of the brain are implicated in self-talk, much like when someone else is talking to us.[14] Therefore, the **power of words** can impact us whether we are saying something to ourselves or whether someone else is saying something to us. In fact, **self-criticism** has been strongly correlated with a range of psychopathologies, such as depression, anxiety and eating disorders, whilst **self-reassurance** is associated with an absence of such mental health conditions.[15]

When I hear clients talking negatively to themselves or about themselves, I often ask, 'Would you say that to an innocent child?' to which they will always respond with a clear 'No' or 'Never'. 'Why?' I will ask. They smile and either they or I or both in tandem will say something like, 'Because it would affect them negatively' – if not downright screw them up, psychologically! If you wouldn't talk to someone else the way you talk to yourself, old or young, stop doing it.

From today onwards, every time something happens that

challenges your resilience, pay attention to how you talk to yourself and use your resilience-o-meter to get immediate knowledge of whether your self-talk, whether silent or aloud, is eroding your resilience armour in that moment or reinforcing it. Just pay attention to your thoughts or spoken words and the sensations they create within your body. Keeping it simple, they either make you feel (a) OFF (overwhelmed, fatigued or fragile), tense, anxious or 'bad', or (b) light and relaxed, or 'good'. From today onwards, the latter is what you are always working towards: thoughts and spoken words that make you feel 'good'.

Belief in Self-Talk

You may be worried that your old cynicism or pessimism will make it difficult for you to reap the rewards of positive thinking, so there is an important question I'd like to answer for you. Can talking to yourself positively still work for you, even if you don't believe in it, if you are willing to try it? Apparently so. In one experiment, those who used positive self-talk performed significantly better than those who used negative self-talk or mixed self-talk, regardless of whether they believed in the power of self-talk.[16] This research also offers intriguing insights into how the brain works. If your belief in self-talk is somewhat irrelevant to its ability to affect you then it would suggest your brain does not monitor the messages it receives from you; it merely lets them in. So you have to be a diligent gatekeeper of the thoughts you let into your mind and ensure you focus your mind, with your self-talk, on what you want to achieve and not on what you fear and don't want to achieve. We don't want to hurtle towards our fears or nightmares, do we? Errr, nope! That would be pretty scary, yet that is what we can do with our self-talk; accelerate ourselves in the direction of our thoughts. That's like willingly driving into a tree or oncoming vehicle.

When my clients start using positive self-talk in place of

negative self-talk, they notice a change in their resilience, that inner strength and pliability, a change in their day-to-day emotions, and a positive change in their behaviours. Much as healthy eating makes us feel less sluggish and more upbeat, healthy thinking and self-talking have similar results because they too affect how our brain and body function.

One question is: Who have you become based on your self-talk diet to date? A better question is: Who might you become if you put your mind to it? Your future self is being shaped by your self-talk in the present so make sure it's taking you in the direction you want to go in. Diane did just that.

Diane S is married with two children and when she and her husband came to me as individual clients, Diane was a full-time housewife whilst her husband was the full-time sole breadwinner. Both husband and wife were individually in a very bad place, psychologically, and very disconnected from one another, and although coaching drastically transformed their mental health and helped save their marriage, let me tell you about Diane. Diane would be streaming with tears through the best part of most sessions in the early days. It wasn't just that she was a sensitive soul who cries easily; she had that feeling of deep sadness, bewilderment and fear. Just a couple of weeks after I introduced Diane to affirmations, with a focus on redirecting her thoughts towards what she was capable of and good at and wanted to achieve, I could already see the difference. However, about five weeks after introducing Diane to positive self-talk and affirmations, she emailed me to say how much she was achieving, that she was not ruminating on negative thoughts at all, and was so happy and so grateful. Suddenly she was lifting herself out of this heavy, dark hole. She was affirming who she wanted to be and by doing so, started to have renewed energy, focus and self-belief. She was achieving more and she was feeling better for it. After all the chaos she had been in, she was finally taking back control of her life and the affirmations were to thank for both that turning point and for some of the progression thereafter. I was so chuffed for Diane and so proud of her.

Our thoughts are central to everything we do and they determine our ability to maintain resilience. Only with positive, self-compassionate thoughts can we create the emotions and behaviours that lead to resolute resilience.

⊨ OVER TO YOU ⊨

Whether your resilience is being tested by an important goal that's out of reach, elements of your life that you loathe, the people in your life, simple unexpected events week-to-week, or unexpected life-changing news you've just received, ensure you talk to yourself as you would want a best friend to talk to you. As a simple rule:

- if it's negative, deflates you, knocks your self-belief, knocks your self-worth, knocks your confidence, and/or sounds like something a non-well-wisher would say, don't say it;
- if it's positive, helps you to have self-belief, helps you to feel confident, helps you to believe in yourself, helps you to focus on your goals, and/or sounds like something a well-wisher would say, say it.

Use the following steps to help:

1. List any negative statements you frequently say to yourself that sabotage your happiness and your goals, and stop saying them. As you identify more, ban them too.
2. Make a habit of talking positively to yourself ALL the time. Remember, do something often enough and it becomes habit.

3. Use affirmations to help you. Affirmations are positive statements spoken in the present tense that help you to focus your mind on the necessary qualities and behaviours for you to be happy within yourself and/or achieve your goals.

   a. Affirmations should create inner ease rather than inner uneasiness. So if you are affirming, 'I am confident' and this is creating inner uneasiness, temporarily affirm, 'I am becoming increasingly confident every day' and then once your confidence has grown, with thanks to your self-talk and ensuing emotions and behaviours, then you can affirm, 'I am confident'. Your bodily sensations and inner critic will instantly tell you if something feels comfortable or not, and use those to inform your affirmation creation process.

   b. Create your affirmations in the present tense to reflect that you already **think a certain way** and/or already **possess certain qualities**, for example:

      o 'I have healthy self-esteem' (or 'I have increasingly healthy self-esteem')
      o 'I am capable of achieving anything I set my mind to'
      o 'I am compassionate with myself and others'
      o 'I am resilient and can handle any challenge life throws at me'
      o 'I always find solutions to challenges, quickly'
      o 'I learn quickly.'
      o 'I communicate well with my loved ones.'

   c. Affirm these statements as often as you can but at least first thing in the morning and last thing at night, repeating each one a few times, as desired. The former will help set your day up with a self-serving focus. The latter will help you to absorb it in your relaxed state, and the statements will also be fresh in your mind so that whilst you sleep, your brain can consolidate them as memories and aim to prob-lem-solve how you can become or achieve those things, too. More on this later.

<hr>

SUMMARY

Our words, whether silent or spoken, influence our minute-to-minute emotions and tell our mind what to focus on and work towards; our thoughts steer our life. Your current reality is a reflection of your predominant self-talk to date and how you use your thoughts from this point on will shape your future.

Habitual thoughts, emotions and behaviours also change the structure of your brain so if you don't consciously create good habits, you can unconsciously create bad habits, however unintentional.

From now on, do yourself a favour: be a good gatekeeper of all that you allow into your mind, thereby protecting and reinforcing your resilience armour.

The Power of Emotions

Within our emotions lie answers, truths and instructions.

Emotions are weird; we can change them within moments by changing our thoughts and yet they can still have such a hold over us and our lives! They can be our best friend, helping us to make great decisions and achieve goals easily, but they can also be our worst enemy, ruining the joy of the moment we're living in and robbing our future of possibilities. This is why working to maintain positive emotions is so crucial.

There are two ways to regulate your emotions. One is to generate inner peace and happiness by preventing anything that sabotages it (including how we use our thoughts), as we have been exploring. The other is, if prevention hasn't completely worked and you've spun 180 degrees towards inner turmoil and unhappiness, to turn your emotions around once again.

Your emotions are your mental health feedback system, similar to the body's physical health and survival feedback systems. The body, for example, conserves energy, regulates body temperature, alerts us to danger via pain, visible symptoms or loss of function, and so on. When the human body experiences pain we tend to notice it, learn from it and aim to prevent the pain or health-problem-causing behaviour in the future. When we apply the same principle to matters of the mind, we use these feedback loops in the same way. **We use negative emotions to know that 'something doesn't feel good' and needs addressing, and positive emotions to know that 'things feel good' and can or should continue.**

So from now on, when something creates emotional pain for you, all you have to do is:

◊ notice it,
◊ learn from it,
◊ prevent whatever caused it from recurring (whether thoughts, spoken words or behaviours; yours or other people's).

Whether you use your in-built mental health feedback loop or not depends on whether you (a) are consciously in the driving seat of your life, (b) are mentally on auto-pilot or (c) have left the driver's seat altogether because you have either pulled over (have stopped trying and are not seeking solutions), or are allowing someone else to drive (have put someone else in charge of your life).

You want to be in the driving seat of your life, steering wheel in hand, present at all times. We all fall into auto-pilot mode from time to time, both when we are actually driving a car and can't remember part of the journey we've driven, and also in our lives when we let things happen without taking the time to reflect and introspect. However, we have to reflect and introspect in order to consolidate memories, learn from life and maintain resilience. If you forget to do this or refuse out of fear of what you may discover and how much it might hurt, then you're missing out on the number-one mental health and happiness tool at your disposal. All you have to give in exchange is a little of your time and a little faith that you'll handle it and be glad you did it. Besides, when you don't address the stuff that keeps hurting, it'll just keep on knocking until you pay attention. It might show up in unexpected ways, but somehow its presence, or manifestations of you suppressing it, will be in your life, e.g. emotional eating, obsessing over insignificant issues, back ache and unconscious lifestyle changes.

When I work with clients who are depressed – some who are on antidepressants, some who have been but aren't currently, and some who have never been – they're always depressed because they are unhappy with some element of their life and they feel stuck in the pain and don't know how to resolve it. Antidepressants may numb the pain, but they can't heal the source of the pain, the reason for the unhappiness. Only the individual can do that. The depression acts as a feedback loop, giving high alert that something is troubling their mind.

Simply put, reflecting and introspecting means we consciously use our in-built mental health feedback loop to our advantage, using it always as a source of wisdom. This very same feedback system is informing your resilience-o-meter.

⊨ OVER TO YOU ⊨

Take another resilience-o-meter reading to identify how resilient you are feeling right now. Do you feel more resilient as the things you are learning and implementing have started to fall into place in your mind and given you a sense of control, or do you need to read on a bit more first? Remember, you're just learning about yourself, being a great student of your life and self, so it's fine if you feel your resilience is still hovering in the same place it was when you took your first reading. Different people experience progress at different speeds, just like my coaching clients:

- You might have started feeling better the moment you picked up this book.
- Maybe you felt more buoyant after reading just a handful of pages.
- Perhaps you've just felt a shift towards optimism and excitement after learning about the power of thoughts.
- If you're in a really bad place and need to significantly increase your resilience, you may only feel better after you have read more of the book, and how much more

will depend on how seriously you're reflecting and introspecting, and completing the exercises.

So again, using a position on your body as a point of reference,
finish this sentence:

'My current resilience-o-meter reading is by my . . .'

Make a written note of it with the date and time. If it has risen,
well done. If it hasn't risen, just be patient with yourself and make
sure you are really absorbing what you are reading and implementing the solutions offered, at every opportunity you get.

⊢⟶⊣

Positive Emotions Change Us

Our ability to regulate our emotions quickly and well goes
hand-in-hand with our ability to be resilient in the face of life's
challenges, big and small.[17] Resilient and non-resilient people think
and feel very differently when faced with challenges, both in a
laboratory setting and in real life. In the first two experiments of
a study, participants' heart rates were tested to see how quickly
they returned to a relaxed state after being subjected to a state of
stress. High-resilience participants' heart rates returned to their
baseline rate quicker than those of the low-resilience participants.[18]
This quicker cardiovascular recovery could be a sign that
high-resilience people frequently face challenges with a positive
outlook (Resilience Pillar 1) and so experience less stress and
worry. In the third experiment, high- and low-resilience participants
reported equal levels of frustration in response to the life challenge
they were describing, yet there were stark differences between
them. The high-resilience participants reported **more positive
emotions before describing their life challenge** and **more
positive emotions in response to their challenge** such as more
eagerness, excitement, happiness and interest, even during their

high level of frustration. These positive emotions reported by the high-resilience participants also suggests a strong possibility that they had a positive outlook on challenges (Resilience Pillar 1) given the thoughts that would have to precede these emotions.

Positive emotions also essentially make us smarter because they broaden the scope of our attention[19] and enable us to creatively problem-solve better as they help us to conjure up more new ideas for handling a situation.[20] Negative emotions, on the other hand, inhibit our ability to problem-solve.

Plus, our emotional state preceding a challenge is at least as important as regulating our emotions when we're in the midst of facing a challenge. Police officers with both low levels of negative emotion and high levels of positive emotion prior to facing stressful events on duty were found to face their on-duty challenges resiliently.[21]

So, if you want to be resilient for the unforeseen circumstances of life, you can prepare by practising maintaining emotional well-being throughout the day. Notice the word 'practise'; maintaining mental well-being is a habit, as is maintaining resilience. The things we do often enough, consistently enough, become a habit. At least, the brain 'programmes' it this way.

Emotion-Regulation Leads to Life-Regulation

Remember, emotions are part of the human body's mental health feedback system, and sometimes it's only when it hits you that something doesn't feel good or manageable any more that you notice the warning and do something about it.

When people grieving the death of a loved one find that 'time is the best healer', is that just because they are eventually forced, by their mental health feedback system, to refocus their mind on other aspects of their life, purely to keep on surviving, resiliently? Those who find the pain of a loved one's passing excruciating might eventually realise they cannot keep ruminating on the loss because the grief is simply too 'heavy' to keep carrying. It's so very sad, yet they know they have to carry on living so they have to find a way to divert their thoughts towards more healthy things and rebuild their resilience for survival.

When something really painful happens, redirecting your thoughts to other (positive) aspects of your life can help you to move away from relentless mental obsession over something that makes you deeply unhappy. Take time to think about the painful stuff – sometimes we have to – but limit it to manageable chunks of time so that, overall, you stay emotionally tough and resilient. Redirect your thoughts to redirect your feelings.

Create New Emotions for Old Memories, Within Minutes

At times, no matter how much you redirect your thoughts, some things stay attached to you, holding you down, day in and day out. Their effect can be quite pronounced; they can cause you to become anxious about similar future situations or they can suffocate your self-esteem.

If you have a general idea of the source of your ongoing negative emotion (e.g. anxiety, anger, low-confidence, low self-esteem), whether from your childhood, adolescence, young adulthood or recent years, you can determine the specific reason by doing a quick thoughts scan of possible causes of the pain, coupled with a body scan. As you consider each possibility and simultaneously focus your mind inwards on your bodily sensations and listen to that voice in your head, you'll often notice one seems to stand out more than the others.

When you know the source of your emotional turmoil, reappraising or re-evaluating that painful past experience (event or relationship) in a less negative way will help you to regulate your emotions about it.[22, 23, 24] This means looking at the event or relationship from a different, more neutral or positive perspective, and making more positive judgements about it, what it meant and what it means about you. We saw the power of this on page 53 with Daniel D. It's a great way to finally release that heavy burden you've been dragging about, albeit sometimes without even fully realising it. Again, notice the power of our thoughts. That we can rapidly change even emotional pain that has lingered on for years and shaped our self-image, well-being and our life, is fascinating!

Interestingly, reappraising or reinterpreting a negative past experience in a less negative way is effective for regulating emotions, whereas suppression isn't:[25] so do take time to fully reappraise past events and people rather than simply suppressing your emotions about them. Your brain wants you to deal with the memory, not just push it and your connected emotions away. Remember, your emotions are symptoms of a concern your brain has; pushing that symptom away isn't going to solve your brain's underlying concern. Deal with the cause, not the symptom.

I had a client, Katherine A, who worked in television. Katherine had moderately low self-esteem that partially stemmed from her adolescent relationships with her parents. She questioned her worth because her parents had made choices (like divorce and new living arrangements) that had affected her since she was a teenager, yet she didn't feel they ever really considered how their choices affected her. If anything, Katherine felt that she was expected to tend to her mother's emotional needs whilst her needs were forgotten, even though she desired and needed her mother's attention. As we together reviewed and reinterpreted some of Katherine's old memories of her mother and father in a way that allowed her to view her parents' decisions and behaviours in a more empathic and neutral way, Katherine was able to release the hold the previous, more negative appraisals had had over her self-worth and happiness. Doing so enabled her to feel much more resilient to any day-to-day events that previously would have challenged her self-worth, and also enabled her to move much more fluidly towards her goals. She began taking proper time out for self-care, speaking up for herself in her important relationships, was more resilient to bad dates, more optimistic and excited about finding someone to spend her life with, and made much more bold decisions about who she'd allow into her life.

Being able to reinterpret previous interpersonal challenges in a more positive way allows us to have a much better self-image, and better relationships with others in general and those specific to the memory.

⊨ OVER TO YOU ⊨

In your life, if there are difficult memories that are holding you back, old or new, identify them and then reappraise them. It can be useful to metaphorically take a step back and look for alternative ways to view them, or to think of the advice you would give a close friend if it was their experience you were trying to help them to view from a different perspective.

Use the following steps to do this and then repeat for each painful experience or memory:

1. Write down the painful experience/memory.
2. Tune in to your bodily sensations to take a resilience-o-meter reading and use a position on your body to pinpoint its level.
3. Reappraise the experience/memory (using either of the two techniques described just now).
4. As you reflect wholeheartedly on the new appraisal, take another resilience-o-meter reading and use a position on your body to pinpoint its level.

Your body will tell you if the reappraisal has helped. If not, try a different realistic appraisal that is more positive or at least more neutral than the original one.

You may not feel a massive positive difference immediately, but rather after some days have gone by, as you notice the difference the new appraisal makes to your self-worth, confidence and resilience.

―――

Watch What You're Absorbing

Powerfully, the tiniest piece of information absorbed through our senses can trigger a quick change in our emotional state. For example, our brain pays fairly automatic attention to unpleasant emotional images (probably scanning for danger) but when we actively focus on more neutral aspects of the image, we can force the brain to 'relax' (down-regulate its emotional response) within roughly half a second.[26] So a great trick to rapidly jolt yourself out of a negative emotion would be to choose where you focus your visual attention: focusing on a more neutral aspect or looking elsewhere altogether, for example, at images of people smiling or nature (real or photographed). This can be especially important if you are imminently about to face a challenge and want a quick 'pick-me-up'.

That's just one example, though. Have you ever used a hot drink to help you relax because the warmth has a calming effect on your body and mind, subsequently altering how you conduct yourself or manage a difficult situation? Have you ever looked at images of cute baby animals to help you feel happy when you're feeling down? Have you ever tuned into a classical music radio station in the car because it helps you to feel less anxious about the thing you're driving to, and instead to feel more peaceful? Start trying it. The mind and body react to environmental triggers you absorb through your senses: what you see, hear, smell, taste and feel on your skin. This is why some home sellers will cook fresh bread when they have house viewings: to create a homely sensation in the prospective buyer through their sense of smell. This is why massage therapists will use soothing music and calming scents: to relax their clients further. This is why a luxurious hotel might use the colour gold to evoke feelings of grandeur and pride within its high-paying guests. What are you absorbing through your senses daily? Be especially mindful of it when you are having difficult moments, but aim to be mindful of it at all times, for it is influencing your thoughts, emotions and behaviours; as we intuitively know, but often don't think about proactively or use to our advantage. Start using this to your advantage from today.

⊱ OVER TO YOU ⊰

What can you use to help you to feel calmer or happier or energised or whatever emotion you want to evoke? Is it a hot drinking cup in your hands when you're feeling nervous or a soft jumper when you're feeling fragile? Would you feel calmer with a more pleasant painting hanging in your office or would brighter cushions in your living room uplift you? Could you save images of cute puppies or pandas on your mobile phone if they always trigger an instant happy feeling when viewed, or should you create a playlist of songs that always make you feel upbeat and ready to take on any challenge?

Whilst this is fresh in your mind, create a quick 'go-to' list now of the things that, when absorbed through your senses, would help transform your emotional state within moments. Finish the sentences below. They might be **permanent** changes like a picture by your desk or furnishings in your home, or they might be **momentary** changes like a warm cup in your hand:

- 'The following things always help me to feel relaxed:...'
- 'The following things always help me to feel happy:...'
- 'The following things always help me to feel confident:...'
- 'The following things always help me to feel energised:...'
- 'The following things always help me to feel empowered (in control):...'

Now you have them listed, set about making the sensory changes that are permanent and ensure the other in-the-moment sensory changes are accessible, e.g.:

- saving a playlist of music that always makes you feel happy in your phone, so that when the time comes you can simply press play;
- saving images of adorable baby animals, or happy memories, in your phone;
- having a hot water bottle to warm you up and relax you;
- having any candles that help you relax at the smell or sight of them lit.

Do the Things that Make You Happy to Frequently Reinforce Your Resilience Armour

The prevention of anything that sabotages our mental well-being requires good habits. Our habits shape our reality because anything repeated often enough has an impact on our lives: whether it's something we do, something we feel, or something we think. The important thing is to pick habits that are good for you and eliminate habits that are bad for you; and to do anything that's bad for you but feels good in moderation, rather than habitually. Unfortunately, we're so busy running around in our busy lives with our busy minds in the busy modern world that we forget this simple rule. Instead, we often end up habitually indulging the bad stuff and only indulge the good stuff in moderation . . . or in minuscule amounts. It's time to address that balance, for the sake of your resilience and for the sake of your sanity.

If we frequently do the things that make us happy, like spending time with loved ones, drawing, carving wood or hiking in nature, we will frequently experience positive emotions and that is so simple and so powerful in itself and yet so easily overlooked. But there is also an incredible side effect; these positive emotions help buffer the effects of life's challenges because we're already in a positive mindset and equipped for broader thinking and better problem-solving.

Even if you dislike one current aspect of your life, e.g. your job, frequently doing something you enjoy in your spare time will help you to feel happy. That in turn may give you a different perspective on your career or life; maybe you'll find ways to make your current job satisfying or get creative about finding a different job or career path altogether.

Equally important is ongoing self-care and minimising or eliminating frequent interactions with those who make you feel miserable, drain you, or reinforce a low sense of self-worth in you. We'll explore both in upcoming chapters.

Researchers have identified four categories of activities that we tend to engage in to increase positive emotions – the more we do them, the happier we feel.[27] The four types of happiness-creating behaviours you need to stock up on are:

◊ **social activities** such as spending time with friends and family;
◊ **recreational activities** such as hobbies or interests;
◊ **achievement-oriented behaviours** such as working on a goal that will create a sense of achievement;
◊ **spiritual activities** such as praying, meditating and worshipping.

There are also a number of simple, quick, cost-effective activities for improving well-being that have been empirically tested many times over. Such techniques include:

◊ writing letters expressing gratitude,
◊ counting one's blessings,

◊ performing acts of kindness,
◊ cultivating one's strengths,
◊ visualising one's ideal future selves
◊ and meditating.[28]

These simple, quick activities are easy to slot into our day, whether we are waiting in line for a coffee or taking a break from our work.

Notice: all of these simple activities angle the lens of our mind in a positive direction and by doing so, manipulate our emotions to follow suit. When we're struggling to switch off from negative thoughts, it is important to distract ourselves from ruminating at length because obsessive negative thoughts also affect our cognitive abilities (such as problem-solving and decision-making), can damage our brain's emotion-regulation centres, and sabotage our goals. Plus, it doesn't *feel* good! Channelling your thoughts in a positive direction does.

⊨ OVER TO YOU ⊨

For your four-week resilience plan and beyond, set yourself some goals around the following activities so that they become a part of your daily or weekly routine – they will assist the maintenance of ongoing positive emotions: (a) socialising; (b) indulging interests or hobbies; (c) being spiritual; (d) striving for and achieving goals. Schedule them into your diary. So you have enough time and attention for the other important tasks and people in your life, and so you become mostly self-reliant for your happiness, here are some frequencies to guide you:

a. socialising **one to two times a week**;
b. indulging interests or hobbies **two to seven times a week**;
c. being spiritual **weekly or daily**;
d. striving for and achieving goals **daily or near daily**.

Examples of activities for each category:

a. **socialising** – seeing family/friends at home, going for a
   meal with your partner, going out on the town, attending
   a meet-up or interest group;
b. **indulging interests or hobbies** – arts and crafts, computer
   games, hiking, dancing, reading, playing a musical
   instrument;
c. **being spiritual** – praying, meditating, attending places of
   worship, reading religious books;
d. **striving for and achieving goals** – learning a new skill,
   creating something valuable out of a hobby (like an
   album or a career), earning a university degree, getting
   married, creating a pension or investing money.

Factors that Influence the Effectiveness of Happiness-Building Activities

Now you may be wondering where you're going to fit all these
happiness-building activities in, both the quick fixes like counting
our blessings and the deeper, long-lasting solutions like indulging
interests or hobbies. But this is the stuff that should take priority
in your life. Remember, in a busy distracted world we need
to ensure the stuff we do most often is the stuff that is good for
us. Recoup the wasted time you spend elsewhere if you need to.
Your social media friends will survive without you for a day
or three. You can record your TV shows to save time on watching
adverts. And if you really need to socialise a bit more for your
mental health, you can probably pay someone to clean your
house; maybe a youngster in the family can even offer you cheap
labour! The opportunities are endless when we put our mind
to it.

Once you've got happiness-building activities integrated into your life, you'll also want to know which factors affect the success of simple well-being techniques. Well, for one, **the larger the dose**, the better it seems. For example, in one study, performing five kind acts in one day, once a week, for six weeks resulted in larger increases in well-being than did spacing out the acts of kindness.[29] Perhaps this is because the greater the intensity of positive emotion in that one day, the greater its ability to positively affect our well-being.

Variety is important, too, as we can become somewhat immune to the well-being effects produced by an activity. For example, in one study, counting one's blessings was more effective when done once a week than three times per week. In another study, participants who performed different acts of kindness every week increased their levels of well-being more than those who performed the same kind acts each week.[30]

Happiness-inducing activities may also create **indirect benefits** in other areas of life. For example, 192 participants were assigned to one of three groups and were made to give weekly reports for nine weeks on either (a) the blessings of the week, (b) the hassles of the week, or (c) the life events of the week. Those in the gratitude-focused, blessings group were found to have fewer symptoms of physical illness than those in the other two groups and spent significantly more time exercising each week than those in the hassles group.[31] How telling is that! Such a simple exercise and yet it had a positive impact on the participants' physical health, mental well-being, self-care behaviours and/or motivation.

We can all spend a little time each week appreciating everything that we have and by doing so we focus on how fortunate we are, especially here in the western world. Some people don't even have clean running water; we just go to the kitchen and turn the tap. We live a life of luxury and we don't even realise it or, at least, acknowledge it very often. Can you imagine how happy we would feel if we all took a little time out, frequently, to ruminate over all that we have to be grateful for! We'd probably be high as a kite. When we stop being grateful for all that we have, our world view and our life fall out of balance. These simple activities demonstrate how the tiniest changes to our routine can affect us. They also reveal just how powerful the human mind is in shaping our mental health, our physical health and the reality we experience. After all, as human beings our reality is in fact subjective, and it is influenced by where we angle the lens of our mind.

⊨ OVER TO YOU ⊨

Whenever you want a quick 'pick-me-up' or want to focus your mind in a positive direction for the week or the weekend, use one of these activities to help. These quick fixes cannot replace the ongoing happiness-building activities that should always remain a part of your lifestyle: socialising, indulging interests or hobbies, being spiritual, and striving for and achieving goals. They are your long-term long-lasting strategies for maintaining happiness and mental well-being overall.

When it comes to these quick-fix activities, use a different one each week on a rotation of four weeks, starting with week one of your four-week resilience plan and continuing after the four weeks as required. Again, schedule these into your diary if you are using them at set times like Monday mornings or Friday evenings, but if you are using them as and when, it can still be useful to have a list of the rotation you are going to use:

a. **writing letters expressing gratitude**, e.g. giving written thanks to a partner, family member or friend, in the form of a letter or greetings card;

b. **counting one's blessings**, e.g. anything you're grateful for: your family, your health, your home, your good looks, success at work, loving friends, a goal you recently achieved, a holiday you've been on, your upbringing, your income;

c. **performing acts of kindness**, e.g. giving your time to an elderly neighbour, helping out at a food kitchen, helping a friend in need, supporting a colleague;

d. **cultivating one's strengths**, e.g. spending time refining your skills for a hobby or your career;

e. **visualising one's ideal future self**, e.g. as someone happy, successful, peaceful or self-sufficient, as a leader who's created a positive change in society, as a person who's achieved a major goal-related feat of some sort;

f. **meditating**, e.g. meditation or prayer, spiritual or mindful.

Nature Nurtures

Although long-term happiness-building strategies are the secret to a well-rounded life, the quick emotion-regulation techniques can feel like an absolute life-saver, or at least, sanity-saver. Sometimes we need quick help to get in the driving seat of our life right now because we're being sabotaged by our negative emotions, so another quick, easy way to distract ourselves from ruminating on negative thoughts is by using nature. There is something deeply soothing about nature. Yet the challenge for people living in cooler climates around the world is that we tend to be shut off from nature, with our windows and doors closed to keep heat in, which also keeps the sounds of nature out. We only have to immerse ourselves in nature – even by just cracking open a window and listening – to feel our body relax. So, do get out into nature as often as you can or at least listen to it with an open door or window, even if just for a few minutes. Wrap up and get out and sit in it, or go for a stroll if you can, even if it's only for five to ten minutes.

Research highlights that even scenes of natural environments have a more calming influence on emotions than do scenes of urban environments, both psychologically and physiologically.[32] This can work with images and real-life scenes, so if you're stuck indoors somewhere with no windows overlooking scenes of nature, and you can't get out, you can save images on your smartphone or search the internet for images whenever need be. You can also add some nature to your home or office with some indoor plants that you can spend time focusing on when you need to. If you can get out at times from a frequently stressful place, like your office, it can be useful to know where local parks or other picturesque walking routes are.

Views of nature can also make us less impulsive,[33] enabling us to make better decisions when we're already feeling overwhelmed by a challenge and might otherwise panic and make mistakes. Therefore, before you impulsively shoot your mouth off at your spouse or drink another glass of alcohol or make an irreversible decision you'll regret, get looking at scenes of nature, real or photographed. As you check in with your bodily sensations, you'll feel tension dissipate and notice a new perspective enter your mind as the lens is angled elsewhere . . . with the help of nature.

The Consistency of Positive Emotions is Important

Life can be full of ups and downs and whilst they can deflate us, it's our resilience that keeps us fairly emotionally consistent because:

◊ we know that 'we will handle it', whatever the challenge;
◊ we turn our attention inwards to our resilience-o-meter to know how resilient we're feeling;
◊ and when resilience is low, we simply do the things that will raise it again (more on that to come).

As a result, soon enough we're back to feeling positive emotions again, even amidst the stress of overcoming challenges.

Positive emotions are so important because they provide many researched benefits to our physical health, mental health, relationships, performance, achievement and more. However, if our levels of positive emotion fluctuate a great deal within a day or day-to-day, we may experience lower psychological well-being and life satisfaction and greater anxiety and depression.[34] Remember how the police officers were most resilient when they were already experiencing fewer negative emotions and more positive emotions? It is possible that the more stable our positive emotions are, the more certain we feel about our resilience, our ability to handle life's challenges, minute-to-minute, day-to-day. Equally, if we're not consistently buoyant, we're likely to feel a little apprehension about what the next day or even the next hour may bring. This would keep us in a near-constant state of fight-or-flight which is stressful on the body and can, I have noted with my clients, create inner anger and clouded thinking over time. This finding further reinforces the importance of making a habit of frequently indulging the things that are healthy for us and make us happy day-to-day, like social activities, recreational activities, achievement-oriented behaviours, spiritual activities, positive thoughts, positive self-talk, surrounding ourselves with loving people and proper self-care. These things reinforce your resilience armour in such a way that you are nearly always prepared – chest puffed out, hands on hips (cloak optional), ready to kick ass. Prevention is the best cure, as they say.

SUMMARY

Positive emotions and resilience go hand in hand and maintaining consistency is important to your own feelings of preparedness, so you must focus on daily and weekly activities that make you happy and help you to maintain good mental health on a consistent basis.

When there are major traumas in your life, past or present, they can have a tight grip over your emotions. Finding a different way to evaluate those people or situations can massively help regulate your emotions, whether by attaching a different meaning that doesn't hurt but still makes sense or finding a more fruitful way to channel your grief.

When your resilience feels low (you feel OFF) and you need a quick fix, tweak what you're absorbing through your senses. If something isn't making you feel good, change it; if something will make you feel good, do it.

Maintaining positive emotions can prevent physical illness and give us more energy or more motivation or both, inevitably resulting in positive consequences for our relationships, career, health and income.

Positive Relationships

'The greatest healing therapy is friendship and love.'
Hubert H. Humphrey

The good people in our life are like unintentional bodyguards who give us cover, stop the bullets penetrating our armour and help keep us upright. Old, young, single, dating, married or widowed, positive relationships are a central source of happiness. They help us to enjoy life and weather its storms much more successfully with them than without; people support us and reinforce us. There is way too much to face in this world to face it completely alone with ease, as we'll see.

We know that having positive emotions before encountering a challenge means we are much more likely to meet challenges head-on with optimism, self-belief and bright-eyed inquisitiveness. One way you can maintain fairly consistent positive emotions throughout your life, and maintain a certain level of resilience, is by doing the things daily, weekly and monthly that make you feel happy and good about you and where your life is headed. Integral to this are the people in your life. Whilst we can use quick fixes, in the moment, to help us face challenges resiliently, an ongoing investment in our positive relationships helps us to maintain our emotional reserve and resilience for the long-term.

Positive relationships aid our resilience because they:

◊ make us feel happy, valuable and loved;
◊ empower us to believe in ourselves;
◊ offer us a listening and soothing ear;

◊ help us to view life through different lenses, resulting in
    better decisions and outcomes;
◊ help us to better regulate our emotions;
◊ help us out of tough situations.

It's important both that you have a social network of people
who build your resilience and that you nurture those good
relationships.

In the modern day I notice the disconnection between spouses,
parents and their children, friendship circles and society. It's as
though we got a little too cocky. We seem to think we are so
self-sufficient now that we can ignore people power. We sit
absorbing the outside world through our mobile phones, all the
while ignoring the VIPs in our life like our partner, parents and
children. We fool ourselves into believing that we've connected
with our friends when we've only pressed 'like' on their social
media update, and we're forgetting about our lonely, elderly
neighbours who need some human contact and attention.

We're also so used to instant gratification now that our
perspective on what's important is a little out of whack. We get
frustrated when our mobile phone doesn't load the internet
within seconds. Supermarkets open twenty-four hours a day so
that we can satisfy our 'needs' at 4 p.m. or 4 a.m. We can pre-order
new computer games to avoid waiting even a moment longer
than we have to. We can pay extra money for a twenty-four-hour
courier service on most things and we can download music and
books at the click of a button. We're becoming impatient and lazy
and we're allowing this to shape our approach to our relationships. But successful relationships aren't handed over on a plate,
or downloaded at the click of a button, or ours in twenty-four
hours for just £9.99 extra. Relationships are up there with food,
water, clothing and shelter and you can't just buy them or trade
them in for an upgrade. You have to invest your time and energy
into them and when you do, your resilience will thank you.

'Happiness is Love'

In 1938, one of the world's longest long-term studies began. Between 1939 and 1944, 268 members of Harvard college classes were recruited into what is now called the Grant Study. Between 1940 and 1945, a second cohort of 456 underprivileged young men from Boston's inner-city neighbourhoods was recruited for the Glueck Study. The men who are still alive today are in their nineties and eighties [35,36] Over the decades, physical examinations along with interviews addressing, amongst other things, their psychological well-being, have been conducted. Given the length of the study, you can just imagine what a treasure trove of juicy, insightful data this is.

Robert Waldinger, one of the Harvard researchers, found that three major themes showed up again and again in the seventy-five years' worth of data he reviewed: [37]

1. Relationships are a lifeline. People who have social networks (family, friends, community) are happier, physically healthier and live longer than less well-connected people, whilst people who feel lonely are less happy, tend to have declining health sooner (in midlife) and die younger than people who are not lonely.
2. It's about quality, not quantity. The quality of our close relationships matters more than, say, whether we're in a committed romantic relationship or have lots of friends; and living in the midst of high-conflict relationships is very bad for our health.
3. Good, secure relationships are good for the brain. They protect our brains from decline and we maintain sharper memories. Even if you're in late adulthood and bicker a lot with your significant loved ones, as long as you feel you can rely on them when you really need to, your bickering won't hinder your memories.

Relationships are pretty powerful, then! Time to take stock of how you spend your time? Quality relationships keep us happier and healthier and, as Waldinger puts it, 'Happiness is love'.

In Sickness and in Health

Another interesting finding from this long Harvard study, as discussed by Waldinger, is that a healthy, stable marriage is important to our happiness in later life. When we're young and married, we're learning how to manage marital conflicts as we mould our behaviours and attitudes to fit more comfortably with one another. When we're older and married, however, we're offering one another support, buffering each other from the negatives of life, helping each other to be less affected by things like illness, pain and disability.[38] So marriage can be an investment in our long-term happiness and resilience.

Marriage is powerful because even if we have no one else, we still have a built-in support 'network' (because spouses fulfil so many different roles): someone who looks out for our health, happiness and survival! We commit to spending the rest of our lives together, loving each other, helping each other, relying on each other and creating unique memories together. Marriage is coveted for these reasons and more. Finding someone wonderful to spend your life with will bring you happiness and resilience throughout your life, so do look for the right partner for you, not just any old spouse will do. Once you are married, there are two ways to ensure you maintain a positive relationship: do your best to make yourself happy, and do your best to make your spouse happy. When both spouses do this, everyone's a winner. Life is good and you weather the inevitable storms together, buoyantly.

Friendships and Resilience

Friendships are a great source of social support and resilience for all of us and an especially important one if you don't have a teammate for life, regardless of your age. Like a great spouse, friends can know us intimately and because of their compassion towards us, they create a safe haven in which we can explore ourselves and the world, something we have to do when life nips away at our ankles or outright punches us in the face. Resilience can benefit from even just one single supportive friendship,[39] reinforcing Waldinger's findings that it's more the quality of our relationships than the quantity that shapes our happiness and resilience. Single friendships provided the youngsters in the study with a place to seek support and actively cope with challenges. In other words, to help them with emotion-regulation and problem-solving, thus reinforcing their resilience armour. Yep, that pretty much sounds like a good friend!

Sometimes, in this busy, distracted world, we can fool ourselves into believing we've nurtured our friendships just because we've connected online but, though we can build rapport online, we build a relationship offline. Remember, quality over quantity, says the research. Quality one-on-one time, in person, should be a regular occurrence if you want to maintain a quality friendship. If you are at a long distance from one another, then video calls are the next best thing.

But what if you have no friends, parents, partner or other support network to speak of, or what if it's unsatisfactorily thin? Whilst you work on cultivating one (with the tips to follow), there are other people out there and as people help keep us alive, well and resilient, they're worth seeking out.

Group Resilience

Sometimes you have to look beyond your immediate life to build a social network but whilst social networks are important, any old group of people won't do. In one study looking at the effects of group resilience on a community-based sample of 357 HIV-positive Australian gay men, it was discovered that those who felt they belonged to a group of highly resilient men were significantly less likely to experience poor mental health, such as depression and anxiety, than those who belonged to a less resilient group.[40] Furthermore, those belonging to a high-resilience group were also found to be more likely to experience positive mental health and life satisfaction than those belonging to a less resilient group.

Therefore, before you spend loads of your time with a support group for post-natal depression, multiple sclerosis, drug addiction or something else, remember that how resilient the group is collectively will be likely to determine how resilient you are as an individual, away from the group.

I remember that, in the early days of my coaching practice, I delivered a talk to a group of people who were meeting regularly to explore their similar mental well-being issues. That was one of the most depressing groups I have ever been around. I remember thinking, if I feel miserable here and I'm perfectly happy within myself, then no wonder some of the group members have been coming for years. I'm sure it would be near impossible to fully resolve those mental well-being issues unless they left that group. So, a little common sense goes a long way. Steer clear of groups of 'Negative Ninnies' and 'Debbie Downers' or you'll be going down on that sinking ship with them.

The legendary success philosopher and motivational speaker, Jim Rohn, once said, 'You are the average of the five people you spend the most time with.' Whether five, seven or three, we are certainly heavily influenced by the people we spend the most time around, often subconsciously until we consciously notice who we've become. Rather than wait for those out-of-body experiences where you suddenly realise how much a certain person or group of people has shaped who you've become (for better or for worse), stay mindfully aware of how the people in your life have you thinking, feeling and behaving.

⊨ OVER TO YOU ⊨

Build Your Social Network
Attend fun, local-activity and meet-up groups of interest, or those that at least intrigue you. Go and sample local life and see who you meet along the way. If you don't like something, don't go again. The point is to find places to socialise frequently with new people, identify the ones you seem to get on with, swap contact details and arrange to meet up. Some people may become associates (people you associate with for fun and leisure from time to time) and others may become good friends or fantastic friends.

Meet friends of friends, either when an opportunity like a party arises, or by asking your good friends to organise some group activities for you, them and their other friends.

Attend functions you're invited to, as often as you can. You have to make an effort to socialise when you get asked to as it means people will be more likely to invite you out repeatedly. You're not going to expand your social network at home. Make the most of the opportunities you have to expand your social network if you need to.

Aim to attend one to two such groups or functions a week.

Nurture Your Existing Relationships
Make an effort with your social network; a real (world) effort. Try not to replace real-world connections with online social media contact. It's not even remotely the same and never will be . . . and you know it. So, if your shyness or fears are propelling you to believe they are the same, that's you holding a self-sabotaging attitude that stems from your desire to avoid short-term pain – but doing so will create much deeper long-term and longer-lasting pain.

Be loving, compassionate and supportive of your loved ones. They will be likely to reciprocate and you'll have mostly harmonious relationships. Be tender with them; our good relationships are one of the most precious things in our life, alongside good health. Be understanding and accepting of their flaws, so long as they, on the whole, treat you well. Be there for them when they call upon you for your help, and when they don't.

Let them know how much you appreciate them. This will help you to feel good (as we'll see shortly) and help them to feel good, and make them want to keep nurturing the relationship, too.

Aim to meet up with any one important member of your social network once or twice a week to once a fortnight.

Aim to demonstrate your appreciation at least once a day, if you live with them, and at least every time you see those people that you meet less frequently, and in between meetings if you can (e.g. with a quick phone call, text message, greetings card or some other sentiment).

Ask yourself important questions, and then act upon your answers, as necessary, for the sake of cultivating positive relationships and reinforcing your resilience armour:

- 'Who are the most important people in my life?'
- 'Do I nurture those relationships as best I can or am I complacent about them choosing to be in my life?'
- 'What might happen if I neglect the significant others in my life, regardless of the reasons for doing so?'
- 'How can I improve their experience of me in our relationship? What can I do more of? What can I do less of? What can I do differently? What can I do better?'
- 'If I wholeheartedly nurture the most important relationships in my life, what rewards will I reap now and in the future?

Loneliness and Longevity

Just as we learnt from the Harvard study spanning seventy-five years, there has been a wealth of evidence that loneliness, or perceived loneliness, is linked to our longevity. One study, looking at seventy research studies conducted between 1980 and 2014, identified that feelings of isolation and loneliness can reduce our longevity as much as other well-researched mortality risks, like obesity.[41] They found that objective loneliness and isolation as well as subjective feelings of loneliness and isolation (even when the person is not objectively lonely and isolated) actually predicted a greater risk of death, at a rate similar to obesity.

Wow! This research not only highlights how important it is that we begin to address loneliness and isolation as a health risk; it also conveys how powerful one's perception – one's thoughts – can be in determining one's lifespan. One might say that our thoughts can kill us. Just think about that for a moment: our thoughts can send us to an early grave . . . Yikes!

The fact that people who had friends and weren't physically isolated were still at a greater risk of death because they felt lonely or isolated, regardless, demonstrates the power of the mind and the power of our negative emotions to affect our health and longevity. If mere feelings of isolation and loneliness are enough to reduce our lifespan, as well as actual isolation and loneliness, then we need to think about how we, and our loved ones, can get our 'recommended daily average' (RDA) of social connectedness with other human beings.

Both social integration and social support can help us maintain good physical health,[42] and frequent spousal interaction in late adulthood can help us to reduce the intensity and duration of negative emotions due to perceived poor physical health.[43] Perhaps one of the reasons a satisfying marriage can be so good for our health, longevity and resilience long-term is that, if as we age we have a slimming social network and suffer more physical illness, we can still get frequent social interaction and social support from our spouse. From our point of view, yours and mine, we see this play out in our lives, don't we? We find that physical pain dissipates somewhat when we're in the company of significant others and we feel better, even happy again, once we've offloaded our worries and stresses by sharing them with a loved one. We also see how much more resilient and proactive our friends and family members become when they've spent time laughing or even crying with us. We need to invest in our present and our future by investing in our positive relationships.

There is a fundamental need within human beings to have people listen to us, care for us, help us and uplift us. Such messages tell us that we are valuable and wanted and that we matter. The lonely person, on the other hand, does not have the privilege of these experiences and may feel that they do not matter, and that no one would care if they even existed or not. It is achingly hard to even imagine that feeling, let alone to personally associate with that feeling. Often I notice that my especially distressed clients are those that feel quite alone, even if they are married but feel disconnected from their spouse. Even just being around other human beings through classes and meet-up groups can help people to feel happier and more resilient. This is where the previous exercise will help you.

I recall a very distressed client of mine, Paul M, who worked in a demanding role for an IT firm; he was miserable when coaching began and carrying the possibility of divorce over his head. Paul was on antidepressants when he started coaching sessions with me, and he was completely off the medication and regulating his emotions better by the time coaching had ended. One of the things Paul identified was a sense that he had lost his old self since having had two children. The old Paul was athletic and sociable; the present-day Paul was not. To address this, he began to be more sociable with work colleagues and, together with his wife, reconnecting with their old friends again. Over time, amongst other changes he made, these social connections aided his resilience for facing life's challenges around his own mental health, family, marriage and career.

We Gain from Giving

We've gathered that people can be a kind of magical pill in our lives, but it's not about everything people provide – their love, their empathy, their time, their help, etc. – that makes them so powerful. It's deeper than that. For example, giving makes human beings experience more positive emotions than receiving, as noted in studies in various environments and cultures, including one of an isolated, rural society in Vanuatu.[44] In this study, children of two to five years old displayed more emotional expressions of happiness when they gave their sweets away than when they kept them. What's more, the children displayed more happiness when involved in 'costly giving' (giving their own sweets away) than when involved in 'non-costly giving' (giving the experimenter's sweets away). It seems we gain happiness from giving, which highlights how deeply connected we feel with our fellow humans, as if their joy is our joy. How sweet is that! This is what we're about. Not war and division but rather love and togetherness. The former make us feel bitter; the latter make us feel happy. The only thing that gets in the way of that connection is a bad attitude, like racism or homophobia, or a bad emotion, like greed. Use your human connection to your advantage: be a giver at least as much as a taker; be there for others and you will feel good about yourself, too.

It's not just about the good times, either. We can also see the benefits of giving in difficult circumstances, even when people are battling things like depression, anxiety and resettlement challenges. For example, immigrants fleeing their home country because of persecution over sexual orientation or gender identity were found to employ several strategies to help them maintain resilience whilst adjusting to their new homeland:

◊ staying hopeful and positive (Resilience Pillar 1);
◊ utilising community and legal services (Resilience Pillar 3);
◊ receiving support from significant others and friends;
◊ doing whatever it takes (Resilience Pillars 2 and 3);
◊ and giving back.[45]

'Spiritual upkeep' was also found to help boost resilience, particularly for those of Caribbean or African background. What really jumps out of this list, however, is 'giving back'. This is important to note because it is something that we are not necessarily taught unless we belong to one of the religious groups for whom charitable giving is an integral part of their faith (e.g. Christianity or Islam).[46] That even a disadvantaged group of emotionally strained immigrants can experience boosted resilience from giving speaks volumes. There's that human connection again! It also further reminds us that giving to our fellow human beings is important for emotion-regulation and resilience. Maybe this is because:

a. the act of giving helps us to regulate our emotions;
b. our perception of, or emotions about, our own challenges are somehow positively enhanced;
c. our perception of our own resilience is somehow strengthened.

Either way, we gain from giving; either happiness or resilience or both.

I just love research like this because it really hones in on what's important in life. Us. You. Me. People. The constant people in our life, but also the people who simply pass through our lives for a brief moment, leaving a trail in ours as we do in theirs. Just think about how nice it feels as you smile and say 'Morning!' to a fellow pedestrian passing you by on the street and they reciprocate in kind. Think about how good it feels to help the elderly gentleman who has dropped his pen, and you're there to scoop it up and hand it to him with a smile. It's seemingly trivial, but it's not. It's that ability to say, 'I acknowledge you', 'You are important', 'I want to connect with you' or 'I want to help you if I can'. You change their day for the better and you change your own. That's the power of human connection and relationships, however fleeting.

Helping our fellow humans is, in fact, even linked to concrete physical health benefits. For example, giving social support has been linked with lower blood pressure in older adults.[47] On the other hand, receiving support but not giving it back, i.e. a lack of reciprocity, has interestingly been associated with poorer self-rated health, trouble sleeping, and higher risks of depressive symptoms in those averaging sixty years of age.[48] So whilst giving helps our physical and mental health, perhaps receiving without giving creates feelings of inadequacy or guilt, which then damage our mental health and possibly our physical health, too. We humans do, after all, experience happy, healthy relationships as those in which there is relative equilibrium in terms of give and take or costs versus benefits.

Clearly, resilience benefits from giving, even when we are facing tough challenges of our own. Again, something about being valuable in the world seems to be at play here. Perhaps a good question for us to always ask ourselves when we're feeling low on resilience is, 'How can I create feelings of worth and value?' Another question might be, 'What can I do to add value to the world, whether that affects one human being or more?' Reinforcing your resilience armour by raising your self-worth also becomes self-perpetuating because the more resilient you become, the higher your self-worth grows. We'll talk more specifically about how to raise your self-esteem and self-worth shortly (see page 118).

⊨ OVER TO YOU ⊨

Write down four small ways in which you can give to others and start doing them.

Pick one a week and do it. Schedule it into your diary if you have to in order to ensure you remember to do it.

For example: have a phone or video call to catch up with a loved one who is somewhat lonely; pop in to see a lonely neighbour; help your ageing parent with the weekly food shop or a chore at home, or just give them company; help someone with a problem, whether by setting up a monthly payment to a charity or being a good Samaritan to someone you know or don't know.

If you think you haven't got time, think of how much time you will save when you waste less of it on negative thoughts, emotions, bad decisions, and staying stuck in life.

⊨⊨

Significant Others' Attitudes affect our Motivation to Achieve a Goal

The important people in our life do have a great power over us so we must be mindful of who is in our inner circle. Who do you spend the most time with and (a) how have they shaped your thoughts, emotions and behaviours to date, and (b) how are they shaping your future? It's important you review this every so often. Do you feel as if your life is getting increasingly off track? Who are the people that are abetting it, albeit unintentionally? Who can help you get on track?

A large body of research suggests that when we have a positive attitude towards a behaviour and believe the significant people in our life also have a positive attitude towards that behaviour, this results in greater motivation and action on our part.[49, 50, 51]

For example, Joanne's diabetes diagnosis is difficult to confront because she loves sugary foods and can't imagine spending the rest of her life watching her sugar intake. The doctor suggests she lose weight to help her condition. As she changes her attitude from *this is so unfair and I am so unhappy* to *this diagnosis means I will finally lose weight and that will make me happy*, she begins to problem-solve (Resilience Pillar 3) to find weight-loss methods that will work for her.

If Joanne chooses a weight-loss method that both she and her partner have a positive attitude towards, e.g. brisk walking, she'll be much more likely to sustain that activity, achieve the weight loss and become happier and healthier. On the other hand, if Joanne has a positive attitude towards mountain climbing for weight loss but her partner has a negative attitude towards it (perhaps because it could mean her taking time away from their family, it could be dangerous or it could cost money they can ill afford) then she'll be less likely to maintain this weight-loss activity.

To keep motivation and resolve high (Resilience Pillar 2), find solutions that you and your significant others support, and you'll have a much greater chance of overcoming challenges and achieving your goals resiliently.

⊨ OVER TO YOU ⊨

If you have an unsupportive spouse, friend or family member, ask yourself questions like:

- 'How can I get my spouse/friend/mum/brother to support me?'
- 'What would need to happen/change for them to support me or take my goal seriously?'
- 'How can I reassure them that my pursuing this goal will not negatively affect them?'

- 'How can I reassure them that my pursuing this goal will benefit them, too?'

Use your answers to these questions (and any other good questions you ask yourself) to inform your conversations with your significant others:

1. Tell them in specific terms what you want, including (a) that you want their support, and (b) in what specific ways you want their support.
2. Ask them what else they would need to (a) know or (b) see happen in order to give you the support you are after.

By having frank conversations we gain the answers that we need, and we can then act accordingly.

Relationships and Self-Esteem

Every so often comes that time when you have to take stock of your social network and why you are maintaining such a network if it is not making you happy or healthy.

One thing I've noticed with low-self-esteem clients is that they seem to actively keep unhealthy relationships in their life, often unintentionally, often because of their low self-worth. They unknowingly let these people ruin their inner peace or mistreat them somehow, almost as though it is acceptable, and consequently continue through life with lower self-esteem than they could have. When they start to dissect how these people actually make them feel about themselves, then they realise their impact on their self-image and well-being. Then it gets exciting because as they distance themselves from negative relationships that don't feel good, they start to feel better about themselves. Life looks brighter and feels lighter. They start spending their time only around those that elevate their self-worth and this then builds their resilience at such a rapid rate that they transform their lives, within weeks sometimes; such is the power of our relationships. The transformation is amazing – shocking, but amazing. I *love* those moments. It's so wonderful to watch someone change their life in such a profound way.

The challenge is, most of us have been raised to believe that chronic issues always need complicated solutions that can take years to work. Fortunately, that's not the case. Decades of research and conjecture have led many to believe that people who had 'insecure' or 'secure attachments' (relationships) with their parents or guardians during childhood are predisposed to experience the same type of attachment in their adult romantic relationships. This theory creates a very bleak picture for those who had unstable or non-nurturing parents or guardians in their childhood. If this were true, it would mean that the brain wasn't rewiring itself based on consistent, repeated relationship experiences that proved otherwise later in life. Given that we know the brain rewires itself throughout our lifetime, this assumption is clearly too simplistic and determin-istic, and researchers in the field agree, albeit without referring to the brain's plasticity. The idea that our childhood relationships determine our adult relationships also doesn't take into account our relationships with other caregivers and other influential people in our childhood, early adulthood and later life, such as our other parent, siblings, teachers, lovers and friends.[52, 53] So don't worry, you're not naturally doomed if you had bad parenting!

In one long-term study, researchers noted that almost one third (30 per cent) of the participants changed their 'attachment styles' – some becoming secure, some becoming insecure – demon-strating that there are factors that can bring about a change in our attachment style (the way we relate to others), for better or for worse.[54] Whilst the factors influencing this type of change need more research,[55] they clearly do exist because people only demonstrate a small or moderate degree of continuity in the way they feel and behave in relationships over time.[56] That's great news and so important to remember!

People with low self-esteem have, for far too long, been pitied instead of coached into making better self-care choices, yet that's what adulthood self-esteem ultimately comes down to: how you care for yourself and how you challenge yourself.

You've Got the Power

I've seen low-self-esteem clients significantly boost their self-esteem by improving their relationships and/or pruning their social networks, and indulging self-care (see the next chapter), sometimes in just a few sessions. Something falls into perspective for them, finally, or they let go of old pain, finally, or a few tweaks to their choices and behaviours, repeated consistently over time, change their life. You can do the same.

You have the power to change your relationship behaviours and associations from today. You first learnt relationship behaviours in your childhood and your brain – through consistent and repeat exposure – will have come to associate certain emotions with certain behaviours. **As an adult you have the ability to remould your brain for different associations with relationships and with your self-image**. You can trial different behaviours and see how they alter the outcomes you achieve. When you notice the behaviours that produce desirable outcomes, you simply repeat those better ways of relating and by doing so, positively reinforce them over and over again. As you repeatedly reinforce those behaviours, they begin to feel more natural to you over time until suddenly, those good relationship habits are the way you now relate to people.

All relationships provide us with an opportunity to shape our brain with good relationship habits or bad relationship habits and good relationships or bad relationships. As adults, we make the choice over whether we habitually reinforce good relationship habits or bad ones, and habitually maintain healthy relationships or unhealthy relationships. We simply have to come off auto-pilot and instead pay attention to how each of our relationships, and the habits we indulge within them, are shaping our outcomes and our self-esteem and, at the same time, moulding our brain. Remember, neurons that fire together wire together and neurons that fire apart wire apart. It's up to us to make good or increasingly better choices as we learn from each choice we make. Your relationships allow you to use your mental health feedback loop to tell you (a) which relationship habits work and which don't, and (b) who makes you happy most of the time and who makes you unhappy most of the time. The same can be said for self-esteem. In other words, what elevates your self-esteem and what lowers your self-esteem, and who elevates your self-esteem and who lowers your self-esteem. Understandably, sometimes professional help is needed as a point of reference and clarity, but other times, someone from your support network will do!

Whilst insecure childhood attachments can result in low self-esteem, sometimes low self-esteem is also the indirect result of dysfunctional attitudes[57] and unhelpful relationship behaviours that result in painful experiences that the person then begins to associate with their own worth. It's about being in the driving seat of your life, eyes wide open, and it's about choices.

One thing I've noticed with dating coaching clients in particular – those who have struggled to find their Mr or Mrs Right and have come to me to gain insights and help – is that those who have low self-esteem:

◊ repeatedly, however unintentionally, subjected themselves to unhealthy romantic relationships that would inevitably, repetitively reinforce a low sense of self-worth;

◊ repeatedly did not learn from their unhealthy romantic

relationship experiences until a mental shift took place after
roughly five years of such experiences;

◊ repeatedly display a dysfunctional, self-sabotaging outlook:
   interpreting anything bad that happens in their dating life as
   a sign that they are to blame for any relationship problems
   they encounter (even when they clearly are not); that they
   are inherently less worthy of happiness in some way; and
   that they are inherently less likely to find their Mr or Mrs
   Right to spend their life with.

As a coach who helps people improve their relationships with
others and themselves, I see that childhood relationships with
parents, teachers and peers sometimes dictate our self-image as
adults, sometimes dictate our self-esteem as adults, and sometimes dictate the relationship behaviours we indulge as adults.
This makes perfect sense if we think of our early childhood relationships as forming a blueprint of sorts for us to follow in terms
of how we perceive ourselves and how we behave in relationships.
However, the great thing about being an adult is that we have a
capacity to learn from experiences. This means we can learn
which relationship behaviours don't work well and which do;
which types of personalities are good for us and which aren't. All
we have to do is acknowledge that we are evolving individuals
with evolving brains and that we are in charge of:

◊ our own thoughts and attitudes,
◊ our own emotions,
◊ our own behaviours,
◊ our own relationship choices and
◊ the time we spend actively reflecting and introspecting.

The relationships we have as adults reflect our inner self-image
and self-awareness and so the goal for people with low self-esteem
is getting a different perspective on how they're approaching

relationships. We have to be constantly learning from life and adjusting our decisions and behaviours accordingly. When we do so, we affect our experiences and self-image. If a certain behaviour elicits a certain negative response in someone, try a different behaviour and see what that elicits instead. If a certain outlook or attitude is bringing you misery, see how you can tweak it to make it more neutral or positive and thus self-serving instead of self-sabotaging.

The question isn't, 'Why does this keep happening to me?' The questions are:

◊ 'What have I learnt from every past relationship, good and bad, about what type of relationship truly and consistently feels good?'
◊ 'What have I learnt from every past relationship about which relationships reinforce a healthy self-worth?'
◊ 'What have I learnt from every past relationship about which relationship behaviours sabotage healthy relationships and which relationship behaviours help healthy relationships to flourish?'

Whether or not you have low self-esteem, global or specific (general or pertaining to one particular area of your life, respectively), remember that some research suggests parental affection in childhood is not even significantly linked to self-esteem once we've become young adults, or even just adolescents;[58] it's more closely linked to how you treat yourself.

One form of self-care is being a great gatekeeper of the types of relationships you maintain in your life. Always and only seek out healthy relationships and eliminate (or avoid as much as possible) unhealthy relationships, because healthy relationships reinforce a healthy self-worth and self-esteem whilst unhealthy relationships reinforce a low sense of self-worth and low self-esteem.

Negative relationships make us question our value as a human being, make us feel miserable too often, make us question our own intelligence, knock our resilience to even the simplest day-to-day challenges, make us lack cognitive clarity and result in poor assumptions, decisions and behaviours that negatively shape our life. Positive relationships, on the other hand, make us feel valuable, resilient and clear-headed and result in good judgements, decisions and behaviours that positively shape our life.

⊱ OVER TO YOU ⊰

Only surround yourself with people who reinforce a healthy sense of self-worth. If they frequently make you question your self-worth and/or they proactively knock your self-esteem, whether intentionally or not, you need to remove them from your life or minimise the time you spend under their influence (around them).

Trust the bodily sensations you feel and the emotions they conjure when you interact with them:

- people who are good for us make us 'feel good', emotionally and physically, in their presence, most of the time;
- people who are bad for us make us 'feel bad', emotionally and physically, in their presence, most of the time.

Actively learn from each relationship, tune into the physical sensations you experience most frequently around each person, and watch the outcomes of the relationship behaviours you indulge, so that you can learn as an adult what you may not have learnt as a child about good relationships and relationship habits that serve all parties concerned. Ask yourself questions like:

- 'Which communication styles work well in my various relationships?'
- 'Which behaviours elicit desirable responses in my

various relationships?'
- 'What are the characteristics of the relationships that truly make me feel happy and valuable?'
- 'Am I sabotaging any of my current relationships because of old patterns I've carried over from past unhealthy relationships?'
- 'Where are the boundaries that keep my self-respect and self-worth intact, i.e. how do I know when a relationship has crossed the line from healthy and acceptable to unhealthy and unacceptable?'

If you keep having the same types of unsuccessful romantic relationships or if you keep hitting the same problems with family and friends, or if you keep seeking out the same 'friendships', then you are entrenched in a pattern of behaviour that you need to learn from and then unlearn! Relearn how to have healthy, happy, fulfilling relationships by actively studying all of your relationships, past and present, and if need be, get professional help from someone like myself.

Positive relationships are vital to your resilience so if you are holding on to bad relationships because you feel that you would otherwise feel alone or isolated, reconnect with old friends or estranged family members with the intention of starting with a clean slate if you can, and/or go out and make new friends, or at the very least acquaintances. Just get around people, and only people who are good for you.

Become Your Own Gatekeeper and Secure the Fences

By applying what you learn in this book you'll become diligent at maintaining positive thoughts and emotions and only surrounding yourself with positive relationships, all of which help you to maintain a positive outlook on challenges (Resilience Pillar 1). By doing so, you help your motivation (Resilience Pillar 2) and your ability to problem-solve life's many puzzles (Resilience Pillar 3). However, there are still some guests and intruders lurking around that you need to defend against.

Some guests and intruders have friendly faces and good hearts, some have pretty faces but ugly hearts, others have pleasing aesthetic designs, and others have 'credibility'. When they come knocking with their agendas, you may let them in and even give them refuge, but they may leave you worse off than before they arrived.

My clients will always tell me how much better they feel and how much more easily they have achieved their goals simply by becoming fantastic gatekeepers of what they let into their mind. Guests and intruders come in the form of well-meaning people, ill-intentioned or mentally unhealthy people, online and offline, and we'll look at some of them here and some in the next chapter.

Well-meaning people
You may know these people as your friends, family members, colleagues, neighbours or members of the community. They often mean well, but this doesn't mean they always do right by you, however unintentionally. They may share their negative attitudes, talk about their frequent negative experiences or advise you against 'dangers'. They might say things like:

◊ 'You mustn't get your hopes up, it only leads to disappointment';
◊ 'You should keep that job that you hate because it brings money in';
◊ 'Get your head out of the clouds; nobody can make a living out of that';
◊ 'Just keep your head down and don't ruffle any feathers';
◊ 'Be careful you don't get too close to that guy'.

Often, these people are talking from a place of love or compassion but they are also often talking from a place of fear, failure and inadequacy. Maybe their thinking served them when they were your age, but that template might not work for you even if it did for them. Also, sometimes these people have not reaped what you wish to reap and so should not be your advisors!

⊨ OVER TO YOU ⊨

(A) Think about the people in your life who drain your energy, enthusiasm and self-belief. An easy way to work that out is by using your resilience-o-meter as you merely think of each suspect on your list. Imagine yourself interacting with them and pay attention to the physical sensations within your body as you do. How low is the resilience reading you get as you do this? Is it slightly low, low, very low, dangerously low? Which part of your body would you pinpoint it to? Your chest, your waist, your shin? The lower the reading for each person you suspect chips away at your resilience armour, the more you need to either:

- minimise your time around them;
- ensure your armour is reinforced before you spend time with them, e.g. through proper self-care (to be discussed) and by using the other tips you'll learn in this book;
- work at changing the dynamic between you so that you slowly but surely mould their communications and behaviours with you in a way that will help you to feel more resilient around them.

When I've had clients do this, it has had a profound knock-on effect on their self-esteem and overall mental well-being, and has given them a surge of enthusiasm and focus for their goals as their resilience has shot back up.

You'd be surprised at how just one important change in your life can have a substantial ripple effect on your outlook and resilience.

(B) Right now, write down (i) who you are going to minimise your time with or completely remove from your inner circle, and (ii) in a sentence or two, what positive difference it will make to your life when you remove them from it or minimise their time within it.

(C) Take a resilience-o-meter reading and again, using a position on your body as a point of reference, pinpoint its level and write it down with a date and time: 'My current resilience-o-meter reading is by my . . .'

Ill-intentioned or mentally unhealthy people

Some people are not mentally healthy but you may not realise this when you interact with them, and so they can unintentionally give you bad advice and share negative experiences with you. Others intentionally convey messages that are negative or unhelpful in order to gain something for themselves, regardless of whether they sabotage your goals or happiness in the process.

Again, your resilience-o-meter will help you to know how you feel in their presence, or when meeting them is imminent, or shortly after spending time with them. Do they chip away at your armour or outright knock you down? If so, there's a lesson in that. Just pay attention to that feeling within your body.

Become an active gatekeeper of what you let into your mind and, like my clients, you'll become much happier, more confident, and much more resilient.

Why gamble with your goals and happiness? Simply identify the imposters and guests that undermine your resilience by feeding negativity into your mind, and either stop them entering altogether or guard the gates fiercely. Aim to allow them in only when you absolutely have to (e.g. with someone you can't avoid 100 per cent of the time) or when you feel most resilient to thoughtfully processing whatever they will throw at you.

SUMMARY

Quality relationships are one of the most crucial factors for mental and physical health and our social networks aid our resilience through:

◊ better emotion-regulation;
◊ reducing the impact negative experiences can have on us;
◊ helping us to feel loved and valued and worthy of good fortune;
◊ and enabling us to feel that we add value to others if we make the effort to do so.

Therefore, healthy relationships truly are one of the best ways to reinforce our resilience armour.

Always surround yourself with those who have the ability to reinforce your armour and steer clear of those who will corrode it.

Caring for Ourselves

The associations we build with our relationships and ourselves can be altered at any time.

For us to feel good emotionally, we have to look after ourselves. Let me repeat that: for us to feel good emotionally, we have to look after ourselves.

Good self-care, or how we care for ourselves, nourishes our self-esteem, re-energises us for achieving our goals, and helps us to feel consistently positive day-to-day. These factors then influence our outlook on the world and its challenges (Resilience Pillar 1).

Ultimately, how we care for ourselves determines how easily we sway like that bamboo in the wind. Self-care gives us a constant layer of resilience armour because without proper physical and emotional care and rest, we become easily overwhelmed and fatigued and easily knocked over.

We choose whether we look after our mind, body and brain with good thoughts, positive relationships, regular exercise, good nutrition, restful sleep, nice clothing, proper cleansing, environmental order and so on. So aside from talking positively to yourself and only surrounding yourself with positive relationships, let's have a look at the simple ways in which you can maintain a nourished and rested mind, body and brain.

Self-Compassion

When you lack self-compassion it's as if you're with a bully, sabotaging you with negative judgements and impatience, making it difficult for you to maintain a positive outlook on challenges (Resilience Pillar 1). When you have self-compassion, it's as if you're with a supportive teacher who soothes, encourages and congratulates you.

The whole point of resilience is that you intend, through trial and error, to problem-solve until you achieve your end goal (Resilience Pillar 3). When you lack self-compassion, you are unforgiving of the mistakes you make and so chastise yourself when you make mistakes, and allow the mistakes to unnecessarily or disproportionately knock your self-esteem. This, in turn, makes you less likely to want to try to achieve goals for fear of undoing your self-esteem further if you make any more 'mistakes'. Self-compassion, on the other hand, allows us to accept that mistakes are a natural part of the learning, growing, achieving process. Welcoming potential mistakes is an integral part of meeting challenges head-on and overcoming them, resiliently.

Self-compassion is not only good for your mental well-being; it also enables healthy relationships. Romantic partners can even notice when their partner is being self-compassionate or not[59] because **self-compassion leads to a sense of care, connectedness and resilience**. Partners experience high self-compassion as their partners being significantly more affectionate, warm and considerate, and low self-compassion as their being more detached and self-critical, ruminating on negative emotions about themselves. So be kind and patient with yourself, and with the world, and allow yourself to be fallible, as all humans are. By doing so:

◊ you'll be much happier,
◊ you'll be much more productive,
◊ you'll have better relationships with others,
◊ and you'll achieve more goals with more ease.

Remember, if you and others aren't allowed to make mistakes then you won't know which obstacles are actually stopping you from attaining your goals. Always welcome mistakes and failures as learning curves and stepping stones that are directing you closer to your goals!

⊨ OVER TO YOU ⊨

Mistakes are a part of life and they provide fruitful lessons, so embrace failures and use them to your advantage. Every day during your four-week resilience plan, every time you make a mistake, do the following:

A. Affirm 'It's OK'.
B. Ask yourself, 'What useful lessons can I learn from this?'
C. Only talk to yourself with kind words and in kind tones.

When we make mistakes, positive self-talk really helps.

⊨⊨

Physical Exercise

When you're caught up in the throes of something that is really testing your resilience, it can be easy to let go of the small self-care routines that make us feel good. I often see this play out with newly separated or newly divorced clients or clients who are experiencing depressed moods. Like them, you may fall into bad routines like moping around the house with creased, tatty clothes and scruffy hair, and stop seeing your friends or even the light of day. It's understandable how you may end up in these self-sabotaging routines initially, as habits can have a self-hypnotising effect on us as they deepen. And sometimes, letting go of it all for a day or two or five is nurturing and feels good. Beyond the initial short phase, however, the effects of self-soothing routines start to take a turn for the worse. As we abandon all the small things that once made us happy, we can sit there and start to feel even worse. Suddenly, we're in a full-blown depressed phase and we're maintaining it by abandoning the small daily and weekly habits that actually make us happier and more resilient.

Short- and long-term physical exercise is, as we'll see, vitally important when we're feeling low, anxious, stressed or depressed. Exercise can be an alternative to anti-anxiety drugs and antidepressants. It also helps us get a better night's sleep as we tire ourselves instead of simply moping around the home restfully. Plus, it helps us to problem-solve, as we'll see later on (see page 183).

Brisk walking is brilliant because it is free, accessible and easy. It also has a magical quality. It can do three things for you:

◊ help you to change your mental state from negative to more positive and optimistic;
◊ help you to shift the physical sensations of anxiety and stress and experience relaxation within your body;
◊ help you to see things differently, have new thoughts, achieve new insights and even come up with the very solutions that have been evading you.

Physical activity has been found to be effective for alleviating symptoms of anxiety, and building resilience in those with anxiety.[60, 61] We also intuitively know that when we commit to an exercise plan, however simple, it helps us to feel healthier, improve our physique and boost our self-esteem. Physical activity has similarly been shown to contribute to overall self-esteem in older adults in long-term studies, partially because it helps them to maintain self-sufficiency.[62,63] Self-esteem, of course, helps us to have greater self-belief, regulate our emotions better, have a positive outlook on challenges (Resilience Pillar 1) and be more compassionate with ourselves and so more likely to 'risk failures' when problem-solving challenges (Resilience Pillar 3).

So that's anxiety alleviated, resilience boosted and self-esteem boosted, but the wonder drug that is aerobic exercise doesn't stop there. Aerobic exercise has been found to be significantly effective in treating major depressive disorder when done for twelve weeks, for at least thirty minutes three to five times per week![64] So aerobic exercise is truly healing, particularly when used with some frequency.

As emotion-regulation is vital for a positive outlook, helps motivation and helps problem-solving (Resilience Pillars 1, 2 and 3), **frequent, moderate aerobic exercise is an easy resilience tool at your disposal**. Aerobic exercise can also be a fast mood-elevator when you're feeling low, and want to quickly get back into an 'I can do this' mentality and focus on the 'how' of overcoming the challenge you're facing.

The power of physical exercise doesn't stop there, now that we've added treating depression to the list. Ongoing physical exercise also assists the brain's plasticity and, amongst other things, increases the size of the hippocampus, a region involved in memory and stress regulation![65, 66, 67]

Hmmm, no wonder we feel so much better when we do ongoing physical exercise if it helps us regulate our emotions, overcome anxiety and depression, boost resilience and self-esteem, and boost the brain's ability to learn and improve skills.

Long-term: frequent, moderate aerobic exercise provides a tough ongoing layer to your resilience armour. Short-term: even one aerobic session can provide immediate relief and you know it because you feel the shift take place as the tension dissipates from your body, and you're left with a calmer mind.

⊱ OVER TO YOU ⊰

(A) Sustain a pleasurable aerobic exercise routine throughout your four-week resilience plan (and thereafter). **(B)** Take a quick resilience-o-meter reading directly before, directly after and an hour after, to see how the reading rises each time. Write your readings down so you can watch how frequent aerobic exercise improves your mental well-being, resilience and life over time. A simple table like this may help:

Date	Resilience-o-meter reading before workout	Resilience-o-meter reading after workout	Resilience-o-meter reading one hour after workout ended

Do aerobic exercise that gets your heart rate up, e.g. brisk walking, for at least thirty minutes, three to five times a week.

It can help treat depression, low moods, anxiety and insomnia, help maintain physical health, self-sufficiency and healthy self-esteem, and boost your resilience. It also can be, in my opinion and experience, a great alternative to antidepressants.

Find an aerobic activity that feels pleasurable and sustainable so you'll easily stick at it.

Start where you are mentally and physically, even if that means just fifteen minutes of aerobic exercise three times a week to begin with. Work up to at least thirty minutes, three to five times a week, of moderate aerobic exercise.

Example aerobic exercises: brisk walking, jogging, dancing, swimming, cycling, hiking.

Keep it simple and achievable. The only venue you require for many types of exercise is your home or the streets by your home, particularly if you invest in a treadmill or other cardio machine: a worthwhile investment given the power of aerobic exercise.

Set SMART goals – goals that are **S**pecific, **M**easurable, **A**ttainable, **R**elevant and **T**ime-bound for every workout session you intend to have. SMART goals tell you, at a glance, what specifically you are going to do and when. More on the power of goal-setting later (see page 161). An example SMART goal: I will go for a brisk three-mile walk every Monday, Tuesday and Thursday night at 7 p.m.

Minimise distractions; prevent poor decisions. Have set workout clothes so that the moment the date and time for your exercise arrive, you know exactly where everything you need is so there's less chance of you getting distracted and more chance of you executing your goal, and at exactly the time you intended. This is as important as setting the SMART goal itself.

A Good Night's Sleep

We all know how unenthusiastic, impatient, miserable, unclear, tired, tearful and slow we can sometimes feel when we didn't sleep well the night before. Sleep is our recharge function and our reset button . . . and we all need a reset button sometimes.

When we're lacking sleep:

◊ it's easier for us to experience negative emotions that inhibit a positive outlook on challenges (Resilience Pillar 1);
◊ we struggle with creative problem-solving (Resilience Pillar 3) as we will see in the problem-solving chapter (see page 174);
◊ it depletes the energy reserves that we most certainly need to remain flexible and buoyant, i.e. resilient.

Lack of sleep affects our decision-making in such a way that even one night of sleep deprivation can result in us making riskier decisions even when we're being vigilant. It makes us biased towards the possible gains of an outcome and less focused on the potential losses we could incur.[68] Sleep deprivation sabotages you by skewing your perspective and screwing up your calculations so that you start taking unnecessary risks.

It's also easier for us to sabotage our all-important relationships, our support system, when we're sleep-deprived. Lack of sleep can affect our emotional expressiveness, hindering our non-verbal communication, potentially causing misunderstandings with our support network:[69] not great if you need their support with a situation or a project.

Sometimes, though, you really just need your in-built recharge and reset button! You know how some days you can agonise and panic over an issue for hours and yet, the next day, you wake up feeling calm and self-assured? Well, there's a reason for that. Sleep helps us to consolidate memories and reduce the intensity of emotional events, helping us to better regulate our emotions the following day. One night's sleep deprivation, on the other hand, impairs the functioning of the amygdala, resulting in poorer memory consolidation the following day and a continuing negative reaction to a stressful situation (e.g. ongoing worry).[70, 71] Wow! It's as though the brain needs a restful night's sleep to gain perspective and calm down. That definitely feels like a bit of a reset button. Sometimes it really is a good idea to go to sleep and trust that 'everything will look different in the morning' and that 'you'll feel better in the morning'!

The message is loud and clear: proper sleep each night is vital for resilience, both directly and indirectly. Be sure to hit your recharge and reset button on time, each night, allowing for enough time to relax and then sleep.

⊨ OVER TO YOU ⊨

A good eight hours' sleep, give or take, depending on your personal needs, is important. If you suffer from insomnia, try:

- working through your mental concerns with a solution focus, in a notepad, before you go to bed;
- physically exercising more in the day to help tire you out and expel tension from your body, e.g. brisk walking for thirty minutes;
- a hot shower or soak in the bath before bedtime to relax you;
- a hot foot-soak in the evening;
- a meditation exercise (like the one on page 66);
- yoga or some other relaxing activity for the last hour or so before going to sleep;
- a cup of hot milk in bed to relax you;
- avoiding stimulants like coffee before bedtime;
- avoiding eating foods late at night that make you uncomfortable in bed;
- focusing the mind on positive, relaxing thoughts, like good memories;
- focusing the mind on thoughts that completely distract the mind from worrying about the challenge you are working to overcome, e.g. something immersive like a book.

Cleanliness and Pampering

Cleanliness is something we have seen linked to goodness and godliness for centuries, both in written texts and religious scriptures, and beyond. However, cleanliness is also a form of self-care and here's why. Whether because of these stories or something innate within us, cleanliness does make us feel good!

Several studies have found intricate links between how clean we are physically, how good or clean we feel psychologically, how clean our environment is, and our thoughts and behaviours. For example, merely thinking of a past immoral behaviour we have indulged motivates a desire to physically cleanse afterwards, and the physical act of cleaning our hands can actually make us feel psychologically cleansed of our past wrongdoings.[72] Hold the phone! That's one striking connection given that the two are completely unrelated, e.g. talking disrespectfully to your loving mum, feeling guilty for it later, and then feeling absolved of your guilt by, you know, just cleaning your hands. That's some delicate brain–body connection right there and shows a strong link between how we look after our bodies (self-care) and how we view ourselves psychologically (self-image).

Similarly, being exposed to a bad smell, being seated in a filthy room, being made to think of a physically revolting experience, or watching a video that induces emotions of disgust can make us judge another person more harshly when we learn about something immoral they've done in their past. So even though an odour, the cleanliness of a room, a memory of your own and a video might have nothing to do with the moral behaviour of another person, that person can still be judged more harshly as a result of disgust at your environment and in your mind.[73] That's pretty extreme, yet resonates with what we learnt on page 91 about how the smallest tweaks to what we absorb through our senses can make all the difference to our mood and outlook. If our judgements of others can be skewed by disgust that we have currently or recently absorbed through the senses, or have merely thought about, then surely dirt and disgust attached to our person and home environment also influence our attitudes and behaviours towards others and perhaps more so towards ourselves. If we are the one connected to the dirt, the brain surely comes to associate that dirt and disgust with ourselves.

Smells can also affect our thoughts and behaviours when we're not even consciously aware of their presence, let alone that they're influencing us.[74] Smells can trigger mental associations we have which then influence our behaviours. This means we can react to our environment without knowing we're reacting to it.

The research in this field highlights how the smallest manipulations in our environment can influence our thoughts, feelings and behaviours, and do so without conscious awareness, demonstrating the power your thoughts have over influencing your behaviours at a subconscious level. Think your outlook on life's challenges isn't that integral to resilience? Think again.

Be thoughtful about what you frequently allow in through your senses from this moment on, as these things are shaping your moment-to-moment resilience. Cleanliness is obviously linked to good and dirt to bad: 'I'm good', 'They're good (people)', 'I'm bad', 'They're bad'. Remind yourself that you are good, clean and valuable by keeping a clean and tidy outer world, helping you maintain a calm and happy inner world, and open-mindedness.

⊨ OVER TO YOU ⊨

Build a more positive self-image and a more open, compassionate, positive outlook, from this point on:

A. Keep your body and immediate environment **clean and tidy** every day.

B. Make yourself feel valuable by **treating and pampering** yourself as often as required. This can be once a month, once a week, or three times in one week if you really need a big burst of self-love. You could get a massage, a manicure, a haircut or new clothing; have a soak in the bath; soak your feet; paint your toenails; shave your stubble, and so on. This stuff is especially helpful to do regularly if you suffer from low self-esteem and also if your resilience ever feels dangerously low.

C. Once or twice a year, it can be good to do a **spring clean** if you have a habit of hanging on to old, worn-out things. Whether annually, bi-annually or as and when necessary

throughout the year, throw out tatty clothes, shoes, acces-
sories and other such possessions that you attach to your
own body or personal environment, for these items shape
our self-image by reinforcing either a low self-worth
('This is all I'm worth') or a healthy self-worth. Start right
now: schedule and complete a spring clean during the
next seven days. It's fun, feels good immediately afterwards and has an overall positive effect on your outlook
as the weeks and months go by.

Nutrition and Diet

A balanced nutritional diet provides your brain and body with all
that they need to function well, aside from a good night's sleep
and physical exercise. When your body's reserves are depleted,
they can manifest as psychological and physical symptoms, and
you can feel sad, tired, and lack mental clarity and resilience.

Raw fruits and vegetables are packed with vitamins and
minerals, and fish, meat and dairy products are also great sources
of the nutrients we need for proper, healthy functioning.

Water, given that it constitutes most of our brain and body, can
boost your energy and mental clarity, diminish fine lines (wrinkles),
help you to lose weight, rid the body of toxins, and can even
produce a feeling of euphoria.

Water and nutritious food are to us what petrol or diesel and
water are to a car: vital for functioning.

⊨ OVER TO YOU ⊨

Have processed sugars and junk food from time to time because you've got to enjoy your life; just ensure you eat home-cooked, nutritious meals as often as possible. You'll feel better for it, your weight and health will benefit, and this daily self-care ritual will become another frequent, subconscious reminder of your self-worth.

Replace processed sugar as much as possible by getting your sugar fix instead from natural sources such as bananas, raisins, dates and honey.

Aim to have a balanced diet that is enjoyable, sustainable and includes all vitamins and minerals and water. It's easier to eat healthily if healthy food is all you have in the house so, just as you must surround yourself with healthy relationships, surround yourself with healthy foods, be it in the cupboards at home, your car, your office desk, etc.

Avoid buying pre-cooked meals from the supermarket.

Get some simple recipes off the internet or buy some recipe books that, at least whilst you're creating this healthy-eating habit, are easy to follow.

Buy a good range of cooking utensils.

Know what time you need to start cooking by in order to eat proper meals instead of caving in to the hunger and going for a chippy or frozen pizza.

When you start eating nutritiously and feel the benefits you realise how much more a healthy, balanced diet properly satisfies your hunger, improves your mental well-being, makes you more alert, and gives you the strength and ongoing energy you need for resilience. You'll also realise just how much more flavoursome nutritious food is and you'll end up craving those foods instead.

⊨⊨

Me-Time

Spending time alone in your own company reinforces your self-worth and is often the number-one way to replenish your resilience reserves. Sometimes there are so many people and situations pulling you in different directions that you get exhausted and need me-time.

Always feeling unnecessarily angry with your spouse or feeling distracted from your family? Chances are you need some time to yourself!

'Me-time' allows us to be 'selfishly' indulgent in a self-caring way. We can have a little time out to do exactly what we want to do without having to consider what someone else might want to do. We can do things that make us happy, benefit our mental well-being and, as a result, our relationships and life. We sometimes abandon these personal wants for the sake of a partner, boss, child or someone else but the brain doesn't forget; instead, we are repeatedly reminding our own brain that we must not be worthy of even simple pleasures because perhaps we are not valuable human beings. Reinforce your self-worth by carving out time for yourself – for your health, well-being, personal development and goals – and your brain and body will thank you through positive emotions, a more positive self-image, and more energy and resilience for challenges. **Your subconscious mind is paying attention to how you treat yourself.**

To replenish your resilience reserves, it's also important to spend time away from other people, their interruptions and their demands on your attention, time and energy. And, when your resilience is running very low, every – little – thing – counts. You can actually feel your body and your mind move up and down the levels of your resilience-o-meter with each little help or hindrance. When your thoughts go to things like, *they asked me another question – I don't think I can cope with another question* or *I can't listen to any more noise – I desperately need some silence*, you know your resilience is near the bottom of the tank, or 'by your knees or feet'.

Me-time is time spent by ourselves in the following ways:

1. Just 'being': like when we sit mindfully in the present enjoying this very moment by focusing on everything we are taking in through our senses.
2. Pampering ourselves as discussed on page 140 (massage, retail therapy, manicure, etc.).
3. Doing what we want to do just because we want to do it, like reading a book or creating some art.
4. Spending some time thinking about things:
   a. Reliving good memories for happiness and fun.
   b. Thinking about life and consolidating good memories for recalling later.
   c. Thinking about life to learn from it: what we have learnt about ourselves, human nature, the important people in our lives, and so on.
   d. Thinking about ourselves and our goals, what we're doing and not doing and why, and how these choices are moving us closer to our goals or further away.

Thinking allows us to grow. If all we ever do is spend time doing things, how will we know what we think about things? Besides, if we feel we can't be alone with our thoughts, then we *need* to be alone with our thoughts.

⊨ OVER TO YOU ⊨

Make a habit of spending time alone every day to rest and have a mini-recharge.

If need be, carve out a specific time of day and place, for you to commit to some quality me-time so that life and your loved ones don't get in the way of this all-important routine. You may have to contract this time-out with your partner and find a place of sanctuary away from the family and all their daily hustle and bustle in the home.

If others want your time or you want to give your time to others, you need to recharge yourself and reinforce your resilience armour by having some time to yourself, frequently. It can be important to let your loved ones know you need this for you to be more loving and attentive with them and achieve your shared goals.

Information Overload – Dial it Down

In the modern day information overload is everywhere and distractions are plentiful. We're distracted from our relationship goals, our career goals, our health goals, our spirituality goals and our life goals. We're also often exhausted when it's time to progress those very same goals. The irony is, we are creating and indulging many of these distractions of our own volition and allowing ourselves to become fatigued by it all.

According to a survey by mobile- and Cloud-testing company SOASTA, depending on the region tested, 75–92 per cent of people reported checking their mobile phone apps first thing in the morning, before doing anything else.[75] They also found that an average of 40 per cent of those surveyed opened a social media app first, whilst emails were highest on the list, with 67 per cent of participants stating this was the first thing they checked, before any other morning rituals. What an immediate influx of information to start one's day on! This means before these people can think about living in the present moment or what's on their to-do list or choose the right outlook for their day, they are distracted and their thoughts manipulated by all that incoming information. Processing this information inevitably saps up some of our mental capacity. Plus, the information you may be forcing yourself to process might actually be making you miserable, just as young adults can experience declines in subjective well-being when using Facebook.[76] After all, social media is a gamble: you never know what you are going to be confronted with or how it might influence your thoughts and emotions until it's too late. The same can be said for mainstream media, with all the negative news and frequent reminders of how slim, rich and good-looking you're not. You might be really great at taking charge of your thoughts and generally indulge positive thought–feedback cycles most of the time but we can also be affected by things that happen in the moment, particularly when we're not feeling secure or resilient.

We're in control and we can dial it all down and just let the information in at an intensity we are comfortable with. We're in charge of what we allow in through our senses, after all, aren't we?

When, for example, you're with your partner in the evening and they're trying to converse with you and maybe emotionally reconnect with you after some time apart, if you complain you are exhausted, is there anywhere you can claw back some of that exhaustion from? Where have you been spending your energy reserves?

We all have a limited amount of energy in each day. Exercise, nutrition and sleep will contribute to our daily levels and minute-to-minute levels, as we can see when we have something that gives us a burst of energy, such as a walk, a banana, or a twenty-minute 'power nap'. How we use our brain also determines how much energy we have each day. When we expend so much of our energy on something like, for example, social media, we exhaust our brain on processing information both during our time on the social networking site and afterwards. We may physically switch off the website but our brain does not always switch off immediately. Often, we continue to process what we've just noted, and perhaps recall things we noted previously and start wondering what someone meant by that comment or that photo or . . . on and on our thoughts go. Later, when you need to focus on a task, your partner wants to engage with you, or you need to make important decisions, you may find yourself exhausted; but are you exhausted from your limited energy reserves spent well? That's the question; and if the answer is no, then you know what you need to do.

If you want to conserve your energy, focus and clarity for your important life goals, you must become a great gatekeeper of what you allow in through your senses. Beware the distractions that aren't serving you, your life goals, your loved ones or mankind. Living a life with less fatigue is euphoric and once you start doing it, you'll never go back. You live more in the time that you're alive; you get more life out of each minute. Plus, you feel more resilient because you feel that you can handle more . . . important stuff.

Remember, these distractions can be things that:

◊ usually make you experience negative emotions;
◊ take your time and attention away from your self-care;
◊ take your time and attention away from your loved ones;
◊ take your time and attention away from your important goals.

Take charge of how you affect your physical brain and body's resilience and your psychological resilience through the type of gatekeeper you are of all that you allow in. Be sure to be a conscious, thoughtful gatekeeper rather than one on auto-pilot.

⊱ OVER TO YOU ⊰

Ensure the amount of information you absorb feels enjoyable and manageable. Your sanity and positivity matter.

When you have a driving motivation to achieve important goals (Resilience Pillar 2), you will naturally want to think about where you can claw back the wasted time, energy and focus you need for your goals. If it soothes you, do it. If it distracts you, limit it.

During your four-week resilience plan, get serious about how you spend your limited and precious time. If there are some things you know you do waste too much time on, set some goals for how you'll change it. Activities to consider:

- hours spent watching TV;
- hours spent on personal social media sites like Facebook and Instagram;
- worrying about things that may never happen;
- worrying about a decision you have made and now cannot change.

Set some specific written goals now, for example:

- I will spend, at most, one hour a day on social media, at the weekends only.
- I will distract myself every time I start to worry about something I cannot control, or have no way of knowing if I even need to worry about it.

Reduce how much time you spend on activities that provide little value but cost a lot of time, energy and focus, and that diminish your mental well-being, consciously and subconsciously, during and after.

SUMMARY

Self-care is paramount to self-worth and self-worth is necessary for resilience.

Regardless of your past relationships and past habits, as a mature adult you have the ability to positively shape your self-worth, starting today, by making self-serving choices. Life is shaped by the cumulative effect of our small daily habits, which over time become huge changes.

Pre-plan things well that seem to get neglected when you don't; schedule things into your own diary, and with your family, in order to ensure that you and they give you permission and time to indulge proper self-care.

All forms of self-care reinforce your resilience armour by replenishing your energy reserves daily, helping you to maintain positive emotions fairly consistently and helping you to have the headspace and clarity to problem-solve your way through challenges. Self-care ensures you are well equipped to deal with all life can throw at you. Being equipped before a major trauma is better than trying to play catch-up later.

Remember, when you show yourself compassion and indulge all forms of self-care, you give others clear signals about how you expect them to treat you, too.

Closing Chapters to Let Go

'Yesterday is not ours to recover but tomorrow is ours to win or to lose.' Lyndon B. Johnson

Stella B, an office worker and trainee therapist, came to me because she was in the throes of a romantic relationship and was finding that her self-esteem and previous relationship history were getting in her way. Stella and I recognised that she was acting towards her current partner with some of the behavioural habits she had adopted to defend herself in her previous psychologically abusive relationship of almost a decade. We addressed a number of things that helped Stella to stop sabotaging the present romantic relationship and her own well-being, but there was still a little something in the way. Although Stella had already made great progress, I discussed the need for her to draw a line under the previous painful relationship experience she had been through, to close the chapter once and for all, so that she could psychologically separate herself from that past experience and completely move on. A great way to do this is by performing a chapter-closing ritual of some sort. This technique possibly works very well because, as we saw with the cleanliness research, symbolic behaviours can change our emotional connection to and evaluation of something and so can help us to move forwards, psychologically.

After some discussion, I struck upon a suggestion that triggered an excited widening of Stella's eyes. She became excited as she said something like, 'That's the one! Yes. I'm excited about doing that!' She was excited at the prospect of closing the chapter by burning all the letters that she had received from her abusive ex. I imagine the act of burning items given by him was symbolic of burning to ashes the psychological hold he had over her, and put her in a state of feeling in control after all the control he had held over her, during their many years together and beyond. I was excited for her! Stella clearly did psychologically let go of her abusive past as a year after our three coaching sessions had ended, Stella was still with the new boyfriend she hadn't wanted to chase away; they were due to move in together a couple of months later.

A chapter-closing ritual can be anything you want it to be, and for any situation where you need to draw a line under your past and start over. If you keep carrying the mistakes, insecurities, anger or some other emotional baggage from your past into the present, even though it has no real relevance to your current personality, character or life, it will have a ripple effect on your current life, albeit sometimes insidiously. Your self-esteem can be held down, your behaviours can become subconsciously self-sabotaging, you're much more likely to keep hitting the same challenges and, over time, to drain your energy, self-worth and resilience.

Here are some chapter-closing ritual ideas to help you. As you try to decide which will work best for you, focus on which one feels right. As you imagine using each one for your intended purpose, attune to the feeling it generates because there's a big chance it comes from a place of wisdom, rather than whimsy, as we'll see in the intuition chapter (see page 192).

Toasting a pact

Make a pact over a glass of wine, hot chocolate or some other beverage. For relationships, a pact can really help you to draw a line 'in the sand' between the old relationship and the new one, whether with your friend, child, partner or whomever. This can symbolise a fresh beginning and a decision to leave the past in the past; it's a clean slate.

How to do it: (1) Agree on what you're toasting to. (2) Agree on what will be different once this pact has been made and why that is important, e.g. you're toasting to never again arguing about old mistakes 'X' and 'Y' or incident 'Z', agreeing to leave them in the past so that you can both focus only on your future and move on from the pain of the past. (3) Agree on a drink you're both excited to toast your pact with.

Writing a letter
Write a completely honest, uncensored 'letter' – a letter that you will never send but instead store, destroy or bury (hence allowing you to be brutally honest). It can be a cathartic act, much like speaking to a friend or professional to offload how you feel. It can help you to feel that you have said what you needed to say, got it off your chest, and can now move on. It can also help you to gain clarity over the other person, the situation and your own self, and how you feel about all three, helping you to move on and close the chapter. Sometimes it's just about owning your worth, and vocalising it to yourself: 'I'm worth more than this, I'm important, this isn't going to hold me back psychologically any more, or even slow me down.' Such a technique also prepares us well for any chance encounters that lead to a conversation on one of the topics, or the overarching topic, of your 'letter'.

One client of mine, Anna M, a wife, mum and waitress at the time, wrote her chapter-closing 'letter' to her father who had been absent and inattentive her entire childhood and who, post-divorce, left her in the hands of her drunken mother who tricked her way out of rehabilitation and proceeded to bring strange men home and later, a maltreating stepmother. I remember how saddened and shocked I was when Anna told me about her upbringing. This was not your everyday childhood story. It was and still is one of the bleakest childhood stories I've ever heard and that relationship with her father was now affecting her relationship with her husband. When Anna wrote the chapter-closing letter to her father, she found it hadn't in itself provided her the relief she was hoping for. Interestingly, however, her father phoned her one day soon after, quite out of the blue, and the act of writing that letter helped Anna to honestly and openly tell her father how he had affected her and her life. Her father listened graciously and that conversation helped Anna to finally leave the past in the past and instead focus fully on what she had control over: her thoughts and behaviours in the present. Fortunately, because of ownership and motivation, Anna is now a strong, confident, beautiful, happy wife and mother, proving – as many of my clients do – that traumatic childhood relationships don't have to shape our adult life.

Burning, breaking or burying something

Perhaps you have items (e.g. a love letter or a necklace) that connect you to someone from your past who has a sabotaging psychological hold over you, or perhaps you have mementos that remind you of some unfortunate past event (e.g. a photo or key-ring). Burying such connections with the past can feel as if we're making peace with something and laying it to rest. Burning can feel as if we're making peace with something by erasing its hold over us and/or smudging out its presence. You can also rip it, bin it or throw it into a river, whether it is a chapter-closing 'letter' or an item that reminds you of a time, place or person.

⊨ OVER TO YOU ⊨

Use **a ritual of your choosing** to close the chapter in your life that you need to let go of. Decide on a ritual that makes you (and the other person, if applicable) feel excited and relieved at the thought of doing it. Just use your imagination.

Schedule a good time to carry it out, a time when you are going to be relaxed, when you won't be preoccupied and you will be energetic and focused, and when you'll have the space and privacy for it. With all of this in mind, set a date and time right now for when you are going to complete your specific chapter-closing ritual . . . and then commit to it.

When the ritual has been done, smile to yourself as the weight is lifted and your thoughts turn to excitement for your future. Then, vehemently focus on and continue to work towards your exciting future goals!

SUMMARY

When the past seems to have a hold over us and has done for some time, a chapter-closing ritual can help to finally sever emotional ties and move us confidently and optimistically forward towards the rest of our life.

Setting Goals for
Proper Motivation

*'Nothing can stop the man with the right mental attitude
from achieving his goal; nothing on earth can help
the man with the wrong mental attitude.'*
Thomas Jefferson

Positive thoughts, emotions, relationships and self-care, and letting go of the past, all help us to move resiliently towards our
goals by helping us to maintain a positive outlook on challenges
(Resilience Pillar 1). These good habits also further reinforce our
resilience armour by replenishing and recharging our resilience
reserves so that we don't feel OFF; overwhelmed, fatigued or
fragile. When we live life this way, life is infinitely better and
makes the presence of the other two pillars much easier. So let's
now address more directly how to ensure you have a driving
motivation to achieve an end goal (Resilience Pillar 2) and how to
problem-solve until you do (Resilience Pillar 3).

A goal can be difficult, but when it is important enough, i.e.
we're motivated enough, we always find a way to achieve it and
the energy we are required to expend often doesn't even enter our
mind . . . we tend to just get on with it and nonchalantly say, 'I'll
do whatever needs to be done.' We have a great power within
when we want to use it, or rather, when we are motivated to use
it. That internal energy for a goal provides a great deal of information about it.

When a goal is a 'true goal', it comes accompanied with the
motivation required to achieve it. A true goal, therefore, requires

much less resilience and is accompanied by many more positive emotions than its ugly counterpart, the 'non-true goal'.

A non-true goal lacks this inner energy force and is a goal we are not motivated to achieve, but we pursue it to please others or when, for some reason, we fool ourselves into believing it is a true goal.

With a positive outlook on challenges (Resilience Pillar 1) and a focus on long-term, long-lasting gains rather than short-term, short-lasting pain, you can tune in to your emotions and bodily sensations to help you know which goals you are truly motivated to achieve. When you **focus your mind and heart** on a goal that is your true goal, and really imagine pursuing it or really imagine it coming to fruition, there is an ease of energy flow, even when stress abounds and there are challenges to overcome. When the goal is not your true goal, however, there is a tension that comes from a place that is separate from the stress we experience around achieving the goal itself.

When you identify the emotion the bodily sensation is connected to, you can work backwards on the thought–feedback cycle to suss out which thoughts are shaping those emotions, even if those thoughts have until now been subconscious.

Tension in body ⟶ Emotion this tension is connected to ⟶ Thoughts this emotion is connected to ⟶ What this means for me and my life ⟶ Right goal/decision for me

Remember, correctly identifying a negative emotion can diminish the brain's fight-or-flight response. You will usually find that your bodily tension eases when you identify your negative emotions with the correct labels. More help with identifying your true goals shortly.

Why People Pursue Non-True Goals

When we are working towards our true goal, resilience is pretty easy considering what life may throw at us in the process. It's as though we are gliding through the air with only occasional turbulence.

When we're working on a goal that isn't our true goal, on the other hand, we can feel as though we are trudging through treacle. As we'll see later (see page 192), our subconscious mind can know something before we consciously become aware of that same information. Therefore, it's likely that this difference in fluidity is due to our subconscious mind knowing that this is not the right path for us even though we haven't yet consciously recognised it.

Why then do people follow these 'wrong' paths so easily in life? There are a few reasons.

One, it has a lot to do with how many of us have been brought up, particularly if you were born in the 1980s or earlier. Opportunities were not what they are now in this digital age and so lots of people have been raised with a very careful, 'Steady-Eddie' mentality. You may have been taught to pick a 'sensible' career you could make money in and told to stick with it. Passion and purpose were secondary. Now, of course, we see that teenagers can aspire to having fulfilling careers (with hard work, self-belief and perseverance) doing something they enjoy or are passionate about. Whilst this shift has taken place, many people have parents and teachers who still very much believe that we should make 'safe', lucrative career decisions; that we should settle in love rather than risk being left single for life; that we should have children even if we really want a time-consuming career instead; and that we should be married by a certain age. I sometimes work with clients who have been raised this way who come to me because they are utterly fed up of the career they have pursued for years. Following their logical head has taken its toll and they can't do it any more; their heart is yearning for a change of direction and their sanity demands it.

Two, there are biological reasons for us pushing towards certain goals that may not be our true goals, like settling for a partner who treats you better than all the 'psychos' you've dated before, purely because you're thirty-nine and you want to have kids.

Three, our family and/or friends may be achieving goals and, upon feeling as if we're getting left behind, we might make some ill-thought-out decisions on goals to work towards.

Four, we've been rushed into making a decision about which goal to pursue and have then stuck with that decision even though it doesn't feel quite right for us, e.g. being made redundant and choosing the next job under the pressure of time and financial needs.

The problem here isn't the mistakes we've made. We learn great things from mistakes and if you're making mistakes, you're probably making progress, too. The problem here is sticking with a decision that was a mistake, long after we suspect we may have done so, i.e. ignoring all of our emotions, bodily sensations, and inner voice or intuition that are trying to point us away from the mistake and towards happiness instead.

There is only so much energy we can muster when we are deeply unhappy, even if we're not consciously acknowledging it yet but are subconsciously responding to it, as might be noticeable through seemingly 'accidental' behaviour. There is also only so much inner peace, happiness and resilience that we can experience when working towards a goal that isn't our true goal because Resilience Pillar 2 – a driving motivation to achieve the end goal – is not present. Your resilience-o-meter's reading will not be that high, certainly not for long; it simply cannot be.

$\rightleftharpoons$ **OVER TO YOU** $\rightleftharpoons$

Use your past to help you correctly identify your future goals:

1. Write down two goals you once pursued for a while before you realised they were not your true goals.
2. What made you eventually realise they were not your true goals?
3. What telltale signs can you look out for in the future when considering or actively pursuing other goals, that will highlight when the goal is not a true goal?

$\rightleftharpoons$

Your Inner Motivation

Goals and motivation are delicately interlinked: in some ways goals affect your motivation and in other respects your motivation affects your goals. When you are motivated to achieve an end goal (Resilience Pillar 2 is present), you more readily set specific goals to help you. As you start making progress in the direction of your goals, your motivation increases because the mini-achievements along the way are gratifying. Part of this inner motivation also comes from dopamine and your dopamine might be trying to nudge you in the right direction.

Dopamine is a feel-good brain chemical that is linked to several things, including learning and motivation. Research suggests that dopamine conveys rapidly changing, real-time information about how much we will be rewarded for any effort we invest in a task.[77] By doing so, the release of dopamine helps us to know which goals are worth pursuing and, when the pursuit is worthwhile, it also helps us to feel motivated to pursue it. In other words, as we work towards a goal, dopamine conveys the calculated return on investment (ROI) we will get from investing effort into that task, helping to motivate our behaviour towards that task or away from it. Therefore, the inner motivation and ease of energy flow, or 'fluidity', we experience when we consider achieving a specific goal may partially stem from the dopamine-feedback loop giving live updates on whether it's worth investing energy into that goal. This would explain that trudging-through-treacle feeling we get when we are pursuing a non-true goal. Again, tuning in to your bodily sensations to decipher how motivated you feel towards a goal will help you to know (a) which goals you have a driving motivation to achieve (Resilience Pillar 2), and (b) how you can overcome challenges to achieve your true goals (Resilience Pillar 3).

⊨ OVER TO YOU ⊨

Use a series of questions to help you discover: (a) which current goals are your true goals and which are not; (b) how to tweak your current goals or set new ones that you do have a driving motivation to achieve (Resilience Pillar 2).

Listen to your critical-thinking conscious mind, your intuitive bodily sensations and your interrupting inner voice. Here are some questions to get you started:

1. What bodily sensations am I feeling?
2. What is this bodily sensation connected to? Fear or self-doubt or panic or . . . ?
3. Why am I having that emotion? What thought preceded that emotion?
4. Am I genuinely motivated to achieve this goal *for me*?
5. Why am I really pursuing this goal?
6. Who am I really pursuing this goal for?
7. What would help this tension to shift?
8. What would have to happen for me to feel motivated?
9. What would have to happen for me to feel more

relaxed or optimistic?

10. Which option, 'X' or 'Y', feels good or right?
11. What are my passions or what do I really enjoy?
12. What are my dislikes or what do I really hate?
13. What are my strengths?
14. What are my weaknesses?
15. What are the values that are important for me to live my life by?
16. What do I want to be a part of my life/career/relationship(s)?
17. What do I absolutely not want to be a part of my life/career/relationship(s)?
18. How do I want every day of my life/career/relationship(s) to be?
19. What/who makes me truly happy?
20. What/who makes me truly unhappy?
21. What sort of people do I enjoy spending time around?
22. What sort of people do I hate spending time around?
23. Why is this goal important to me?
24. How would I feel if I didn't achieve this goal?
25. What would happen if I didn't achieve this goal?
26. Is this goal a nice-to-have or a must-have?
27. Does this goal just need tweaking to make it a true goal and if so, how?

How Goals Affect our Performance and Achievement

If you have never really been convinced of the power of goal-setting, this is especially for you. In a review of empirical goal-setting research spanning thirty-five years, researchers summarised four main mechanisms through which goals affect us.[78]

First, goals direct our mental attention and physical behaviours towards activities that will help us to achieve them and away from activities that are irrelevant to achieving them. So, setting a specific goal stops us wasting our time, energy and focus on other pursuits and helps us to more quickly achieve our goals. This is likely to explain why affirmations help: because they can keep us focused on and moving towards the affirmed statement, or goal. This may also explain one way in which reviewing our goals frequently, whether as written goal statements or images depicting the goals, helps us to achieve those very goals.

Second, goals that stretch us lead to more effort than goals that don't. Perhaps this is because we know that a higher goal will require more effort than lower goals. Perhaps this is also because higher goals make us feel more excited than goals that are easy to reach, possibly because we attach our own worth and confidence to the obtainment of the goal, i.e. the bigger the goal, the prouder you'll be of yourself for achieving it and the more confidence you'll have.

Third, goals affect our persistence. When given the choice, we will work longer on a difficult task than on an easy task. We will also work faster when we have tight deadlines than when we have loose deadlines. This again demonstrates that goals influence our focus and behaviour.

Fourth, goals affect our behaviour indirectly. Goals propel us to discover information and strategies that will help us to achieve our objectives.

I always say to my clients that **when we keep a specific goal at the forefront of our mind** via affirmations and goal reminders (e.g. vision boards, goal statements or visualisation – see page 168) our brain is reminded to: (a) **spot**, (b) **grasp** and (c) **create** opportunities to make those goals a reality. It's also why it is so important to always focus your mind on what you do want, not on what you don't want. As I often say, whatever we focus our mind on, we consciously and subconsciously work towards. A large body of research supports this and helps explain why things like affirmations, vision boards and written descriptions help move us towards our goals. These constant reminders of our goals influence our thoughts, behaviours and motivation – as do goals themselves – both directly and indirectly.

Setting Realistic Goals

Goals for the future distract us from worry and anger about the past and redirect our focus to the direction we're travelling in. So, let's define goal-setting. This is the best definition I've ever come across, written in a review of over a decade of research, published in a peer-reviewed academic journal. Goals affect our performance by:

a. directing our attention towards them;
b. preparing us to take action in their direction;
c. increasing our persistence;
d. and motivating us to develop a strategy.[79]

This also highlights why our **goals must be defined in terms of what we want** and not in terms of what we don't want. So, not 'I don't want to fight with my partner all the time,' but instead, 'I want my partner and I to get on well most of the time.'

Proper goal-setting focuses our mind in the right direction and helps ensure we achieve the goal. To achieve the goal, we need to maintain resilience in the face of challenges in its path. The more realistic the goal, the more resilience we will have. So let us explore how we set realistic goals.

Even if it gives you a temporary feeling of confidence, excitement and worth when you set yourself a goal that stretches you massively, if it's an unrealistic goal, the high will be short-lived. Reality will soon set in when you realise it is unachievable and you'll begin to experience different emotions like insecurity, apprehension and self-hate. If you do this over and over, you can falsely begin to believe that you are a procrastinator by nature and that you never achieve goals you set your sights on. Don't set yourself up for failure and negative associations with yourself with an unrealistic goal; set yourself up for success (and self-love) with a realistic goal.

One of my clients, Hayley C, came to me to lose weight and work on her confidence in the workplace. Hayley was fifty-five years old, had been in a very high-powered managerial role for a large local council, and was now working in a small office doing a job that was well below her ability but matched the intensity she wanted at this juncture in her life. Incidentally, Hayley is another client who proved to me that poor childhood and young adulthood relationships do not always shape one's relationships in later life. Hayley and her husband clearly loved each other very deeply and Hayley wanted to ensure she would stay healthy to enjoy life with him. The challenge for Hayley was that she was significantly overweight and she needed a good plan for losing a few stone.

Below are a few of the important factors Hayley and I discussed:

1. The importance of setting goals that stretched her but would be achievable (because we have to believe it's possible to achieve the goal in order to achieve it).[80]
2. The exercise of choice for weight loss needed to be something enjoyable so that she would stick with it easily.
3. Hayley wanted accessible motivational boosts that would help her to stay on track when she could feel her motivation and focus waning.
4. She needed an eating plan that felt easy and achievable, too.
5. She would have to be patient with herself as she rewired her brain for better eating and exercising habits after spending years automating unhelpful habits.

When I saw Hayley for the second session, I was so proud of her progress. In the space of exactly three weeks since our previous session, she had lost a significant amount of weight and could fit into the chair comfortably, which she hadn't been able to do in the session before when I had duly offered a chair without armrests. I was so happy for her and she was happy for herself. She looked so much healthier and perkier and this was just the start.

This highlights what I have seen happen with lots of clients, with varied goals, and what you can achieve when you set realistic goals (both in terms of what you will achieve in a certain time-frame and how), have an accessible source for refocusing and increasing your motivation, and have patience with yourself so you don't expect too much of yourself, too soon.

Every time you set an unachievable goal, you experience negative emotions such as anxiety and pessimism and, as a result, low resilience. This will then influence your behaviours and the results you achieve, or don't achieve, and all so unnecessarily.

Setting realistic goals doesn't mean that we shouldn't think big and aim high for the big goals; it simply means each step of the way should be achievable. So if you're aiming for a big goal, like Hayley, break it down into smaller 'stepping-stone' goals that feel achievable.

It can also be a good idea to reward yourself in small, simple, healthy ways when you achieve those stepping-stone goals and do the same when you achieve your ultimate goal. Predetermining what these rewards will be can help you to work hard towards the goal, especially when it is a difficult one. The reward thus becomes both a distraction and a motivation; sometimes it's easier and more emotionally uplifting to switch your focus from the arduous journey to the reward for its completion.

When you achieve the smaller stepping-stone goals en route to achieving the ultimate goal, you simultaneously build your confidence, which helps transform your self-image and increase your resilience.

Your self-image is how you perceive yourself. The more goals you achieve, the more capable you feel. The more weight you lose and the more dress sizes you drop, the more capable you feel of dropping another dress size. The better you become at dealing with problems at home, the more capable you feel of dealing with any future family issues. Feeling capable is extremely important for building your resilience, so prove to yourself that you are capable by setting yourself realistic goals.

Setting Specific Goals

Earlier we discussed SMART goals (goals that are Specific, Measurable, Attainable, Relevant and Time-bound) but did you know that SMART goals are also scientifically proven to be effective? Remember my example of a SMART goal: 'I will go for a brisk three-mile walk every Monday, Tuesday and Thursday night at 7 p.m.' SMART goals tell you, at a glance, what specifically you are going to do and when or by when.

One study clearly shows that specific 'implementation intentions', or SMART goals (e.g. 'I intend to perform goal-directed behaviour "Y" when I encounter situation "Z"') rather than vague 'goal intentions' (e.g. 'I intend to achieve "X"') result in difficult goals being achieved about three times more often.[81] Plus, specific implementation intentions (SMART goals) help us to immediately do what we say we will do (behaviour 'Y') when the specified time or situation arises (situation 'Z').

The research highlights how SMART goals act as powerful self-regulatory tools that help us overcome typical obstacles preventing us from taking action in the direction of our goals, such as when we're feeling distracted or tired, or want to pursue alternative fun choices instead. Imagine you have a SMART goal that says you're to leave for the gym at 6 p.m. this evening. When a friend phones for a chat at 6 p.m., you are much more likely to speak to them en route to the gym, rather than delay departure, or ask your friend if you can chat another time instead. If you have an implementation intention, or a SMART goal, that says you're going to indulge a certain self-care activity every Sunday at 9 p.m., you'll be much more likely to ensure it happens even when faced with distractions.

The lesson here is that if something is important to you, help yourself to regulate your own behaviours in the direction of your goals by creating SMART goals.

⊨ OVER TO YOU ⊨

1. List every realistic goal you want to achieve during your four-week resilience plan whilst you're training your brain to respond to every challenge with resilience. These might be end goals and/or stepping-stone goals.
2. For each end goal, write down why you are truly motivated to achieve it (why it's 100 per cent a true goal).
3. For every important goal that you want to achieve (end goal and/or stepping stone), create a written SMART goal, e.g.:
   - I will have changed my career to 'X' by (date-month-year).
   - Every Monday and Wednesday between 7 p.m. and 9 p.m., I will attend the local _____ course to qualify as a _____.
   - Every Saturday between 11 a.m. and 12 p.m., I will work as a volunteer at the local _____ to gain work experience for my future career.

Remember, good goals tell us, at a glance, what specifically we are going to do or achieve and when or by when.

Also remember – whether in your mind, on paper or aloud to someone else – that if you're discussing goals or changes, only ever talk in terms of what you do want.

Goals and Emotions

Research shows that the process of striving for goals is in itself important to our mental health, in addition to achieving them,[82] probably because it keeps us challenging ourselves, learning how to overcome challenges resiliently and proving our abilities to ourselves. So emotion-regulation helps us to maintain a positive outlook on challenges (Resilience Pillar 1) and achieve our goals, but striving for goals also helps regulate our emotions, which in turn help us to have a positive outlook on our challenges (Resilience Pillar 1). Maxwell Maltz, a cosmetic surgeon, university lecturer and renowned author, once astutely said, 'Man maintains his balance, poise, and sense of security only as he is moving forward.' When you're not constantly moving forwards, your emotions will suffer.

Interestingly, this research also suggests that higher (difficult) goals do not make us feel any more exhausted than lower (easy) goals, even though we may be exerting more effort. Perhaps this signals how adaptive our brain and body are whenever we set our sights on a goal. It really doesn't matter how difficult the goal is, as long as it is achievable and we are motivated to attain it, our brain and body will muster the resources and knowledge required to achieve it, somewhat effortlessly. In fact, when the goal is one we're truly motivated to achieve, it always feels fairly easy and effortless.

⊱═ OVER TO YOU ═⊰

When motivation for your genuine goals is dwindling, use effective strategies to frequently refocus your mind and re-energise yourself with excitement and self-belief so you move much more swiftly and effortlessly towards your goals! Here are some ways to do this.

Create and frequently view a 'goals poster' or 'vision board' with images and words depicting your goals. For example, a picture of the type of car or house you want to own, or someone in a wedding dress with a cut-out of your face stuck to it, or someone with your colour and style of hair having a massage, or a suit or handbag you want to buy, or a holiday destination you want to take your family to. Simply cut images from magazines or print them off the internet. Every time you look at your collage you remind your brain of the specific, clear goals you want it to work towards. Doing so keeps the 'instruction' to achieve these specific goals at the forefront of your conscious and subconscious mind so that you (a) **spot**, (b) **grasp** and (c) **create** opportunities to make your goals a reality by propelling you towards thoughts, emotions and behaviours that will help you to do so. Our subconscious mind is where a lot of our brain's work is taking place; work that we're not aware of.

Place the poster or board somewhere you will see it frequently, so that you consciously and subconsciously absorb the goal reminders over and over again. Consciously look at your board daily; first thing in the morning or last thing at night, or both. The morning reminder of your goals can help your brain to remember to focus on it during the day. The night-time reminder can help your brain to consolidate your goals and problem-solve how you are going to achieve them as you sleep. More on this in the next chapter (see page 174).

Talk positively to yourself using statements to affirm thoughts and qualities that will build motivation and self-belief. These will become self-fulfilling prophecies through the impact your thoughts will have on your (conscious and subconscious) emotions and behaviours, e.g. 'I can achieve goal "X", easily'; 'I am excited about goal "X"'; 'Pursuing goal "X" is improving my skills'; 'I am good at . . .'; 'The answer is coming to me'.

Use YouTube videos of other people successfully achieving those same (or similar) goals to motivate you to keep striving resiliently through the challenges. Also watch videos that give you valuable information on how they overcame the challenges you are facing.

Access motivating images that depict your goals, via your phone or computer, as a portable version of your goals poster or vision board. You can store images on your phone as and when you find motivational ones, and you can search the internet for such images as and when you need a pick-me-up, if you do not have any relevant ones stored or need new images to reignite your enthusiasm. Make sure they are pleasant depictions of your goals, not unpleasant images of what you are trying to avoid; always focus your mind on what you do want, i.e. the goal, not the fear or the undesirable. You want to instil excitement and focus, not physiological and psychological anxiety and stress.

Visualise your future self once you have achieved your goal, in every detail, including what you are taking in through all five senses (e.g. what you can hear someone saying, the breeze you can feel on your skin, how happy the other person looks, etc.) as well as imagining the emotions you are feeling. Visualising our future selves helps regulate our emotions, as we learnt on pages 94 and 99. It helps us to focus excitedly on our goals and re-energises us to put effort into achieving them. It helps us to create a clear, life-like video of the goal we're working towards, providing clearer instructions for the brain. It also helps the goal to feel believable and when we believe something is possible, *then* we can achieve it.

Get support from your significant others like your partner, family, friends and/or colleagues. If you have no such person you can ask, a professional could help, or a support group or meet-up group, so long as they are a resilient group! For example, you could get:

- practical help with household duties or childcare;
- psychological support when you need help putting your ideas into action plans;
- emotional support when you need uplifting and reassuring.

Motivation comes from within, and sometimes external sources such as those listed here can help. The ultimate question to ask yourself until you receive the correct answer is, 'What can I do to increase my motivation?' Listen to your intuition and take action.

Resilience Pillar 2 – A Driving Motivation – Must be Present

Remember, Resilience Pillar 2 (a driving motivation to achieve an end goal) is a must in order for you to be resilient. As per the exercise on page 160, ask yourself a series of questions and use your brain and body to work out whether your goal is one you have a driving motivation to achieve, i.e. Resilience Pillar 2 is present.

If Resilience Pillar 2 is not present because it is not a true goal, problem-solve until you work out what goal would be a true goal.

If Resilience Pillar 2 is present because it is a true goal, but you're still not feeling resilient, then something is knocking your resilience and you just need to work out what. Perhaps one or more of these is responsible:

◊ Resilience Pillar 1 is missing and so your outlook is sabotaging you;
◊ Resilience Pillar 3 is missing and so you are not problem-solving to achieve the end goal;
◊ you are sabotaging yourself with habitual negative thoughts;
◊ you lack proper self-care;
◊ you need to re-evaluate the past in a better way, or close the chapter on it in some other way, to release its hold over you;
◊ you are currently lacking the skills you require;

◊ you are currently lacking healthy self-esteem;
◊ you are currently lacking confidence / self-belief;
◊ your time-frame for achieving the goal is unrealistic;
◊ your significant others aren't supporting your goal-seeking behaviours or the goal itself;
◊ you spend too much time around people who keep your resilience low;
◊ you allow too much negativity in through your senses;
◊ you're not taking emotion-regulation seriously enough;
◊ you have a competing goal that is vying for your attention but seems mutually exclusive.

When our resilience is wavering, we either need to **alter** something to ensure we achieve our goal or **acknowledge** that it isn't a goal we want to achieve, and then have the guts to pursue what would make us happy instead.

As you consider each goal you think you want to pursue, each goal you believe is important to you, instead of thinking, **feel**. Feel which one has the least resistance. **Follow the energy where it flows, as though it is pulling you rather than you pushing yourself.** This flow of energy will come in very useful as you problem-solve to deal with any obstacles in the path of you, your goals, your happiness and your life purpose.

SUMMARY

Goal-setting directs our attention and behavioural effort, compels us to take action, and helps us to maintain persistence as we strive for our goals, happiness and life purpose.

Remember, goals help us to **spot**, **grasp** and **create** opportunities to achieve our goals. Therefore, frequently focusing the mind in a solution- and goal-focused direction reinforces our resilience armour, helping us to swiftly overcome challenges obstructing us.

Our self-image directly influences our behaviour and so by setting realistic goals and achieving them, we frequently improve our self-image, well-being and confidence, and reinforce our resilience armour.

Your body, ever the purveyor of knowledge, will help you to make the right decisions, focus on the right goals for you and achieve them in the right way, if you will just listen to what it has to say. More on this in the intuition chapter.

Creative Problem-Solving

*'If you wish to find, you must search. Rarely does a good idea
interrupt you.' Jim Rohn*

I love Jim Rohn's way of putting things. We can't sit around
waiting for answers to our problems to magically appear; we have
to strive to find them. How often do you search high and low, in
every nook and cranny, to find the answers to your woes, the
answers that will eventually make everything OK? We have to
search, and you know what, guys and girls? When you are relentless in your search, you will find the solutions.

One day the upcoming problem-solving strategies may not
make much of a difference for you; another day you might
struggle to write down your ideas fast enough! That's the thing
with problem-solving. So many factors can affect it that you just
have to persist; some problem-solving sessions will be fruitful and
others won't be. It's all important work, though, because
sometimes just one great idea can change your life.

Once you have a positive outlook on challenges (Resilience
Pillar 1) and a driving motivation to achieve your end goals
(Resilience Pillar 2), resilience requires goal-serving behaviours
or actions because it's through our actions that we propel
ourselves forward, overcome obstacles and achieve our goals. To
take that leap from genuine desire to successfully overcoming
the challenge, we sometimes know exactly which actions we
need to take, but other times we are unsure or have no idea. This
is where Resilience Pillar 3, a problem-solving approach, comes
into use.

Remember that Resilience Pillar 1 means you bring a positive attitude to the challenges in your way, and this then has a self-serving knock-on effect. It means you keep moving towards your goals, instead of stopping in your tracks when you hit obstacles. You feel positive emotions like optimism and self-belief, and take control of your own destiny as you proactively search for any lessons and other benefits the challenge offers. All of this helps you to be a great problem-solver.

When the same challenge keeps showing up in our lives, it's because we haven't yet learnt all that it is trying to teach us. We see this clearly:

◊ in the people who repeatedly seek out the same types of destructive romantic relationships;
◊ when someone keeps pursuing a career path that makes them miserable;
◊ when someone keeps having the same argument with their beloved.

Honouring the Three Pillars of Resilience enables us to become serious students of our own lives as we optimistically learn from every obstacle we face and use that information to our advantage as we continuously and buoyantly proceed towards our goals and happiness.

To feel as though we can't problem-solve is to feel utterly vulnerable and incapable, and can often be the root of long-term depression. Talk about a resilience-o-meter reading by your knees or below! That's where seeking out a professional, or a book like this one, can help when your view is so obscured that you feel utterly lost in the wilderness that is your mind. So let's simplify this, too!

Creative Problem-Solving Strategies

The best problem-solving strategies that I suggest clients use – and also encourage indirectly through exercises I offer – can be divided into five simple categories: good questions, brainstorming, physical movement, manipulating your perspective, and daydreaming. All five are surprisingly simple and highly effective. All five require patience, resolve and time. Problem-solving is always a work-in-progress and must be treated as such.

Sometimes the answers we're searching for come to us immediately; other times they evade us for weeks. Just trust in the process. If you keep searching for the answers, they invariably present themselves to you at some point, whether after minutes, days or weeks.

If you really commit to proper problem-solving during your four-week journey to a resilient you, you'll find yourself making massive strides forward, achieving some of your important goals outright or being well on your way to doing so. Four weeks is an incredible amount of time. After all, there are only thirteen sets of four weeks in a whole year! You can achieve a lot in four weeks.

When you spend some time focusing on how you can overcome the challenges you are facing, you will notice that your subconscious mind continues problem-solving 'in the background'. This is how answers suddenly pop into your mind when you're not even consciously thinking about the problem or your goal. Maybe you're washing the dishes or ironing some clothes and suddenly, unrelated to your current conscious thoughts, an epiphany enters your mind and gives you new food for thought or actual solutions and answers. Interestingly, the brain also problem-solves whilst we sleep.[83] So if our brain is problem-solving when we are asleep and subconsciously problem-solving when we are awake but not consciously thinking about the problem (as we will see shortly), then it stands to reason that what we feed the mind is of great importance to resiliently and rapidly overcoming challenges.

Common sense also dictates that the brain can only process, and creatively play with, information it has access to, whether consciously or subconsciously. So it can be useful to allow new information to enter through the senses. For this reason, I always recommend that clients who are feeling stuck in a mental rut get out and experience new things, and change their routine. Something new in, something new out. New things for the brain to creatively play with.

The Problem and the Goal

Problem-solving requires that we:

a. clearly know what the problem is ('A'),
b. clearly know what the goal is ('B'), and
c. search for the answers we need to move us from 'A' to 'B' until we have succeeded.

That's it. That is problem-solving in a nutshell. Coaching – whatever type of client I am working with – is all about problem-solving. The same goes for maintaining resilience; it's ultimately just problem-solving to overcome any challenge or obstacle in our life, or life's puzzles.

Charles Kettering's aforementioned statement, 'A problem well-stated is a problem half-solved', suggests that a large and vital part of successful problem-solving is to clearly know what the problem is. Albert Einstein is thought to have said, 'If you can't explain it to a six-year-old, you don't understand it yourself.' That's a powerful statement because it suggests that our ability to clearly and simply communicate something to ourselves or someone else demonstrates if we understand it. If we don't understand it, how can we solve it? It's obvious when we look at it in that way, isn't it?

So we have to be very clear on what the problem is, in very

basic terms: you can test your true understanding of your challenge by writing it down in a simple sentence or two. Once you've done that, you're well on your way to successfully problem-solving it, so long as you fulfil the other problem-solving actions too. If at first you struggle to summarise your challenge in a sentence or two, just write a paragraph and then keep reading it and editing it down until it is one or two sentences.

The brain requires the starting point 'A' and destination 'B' to tune in to its 'sat-nav'. Then, the route to follow reveals itself as you employ the five upcoming solution-finding strategies, and reflect, introspect, take action in the direction of your goals, use what you learn to further reflect, introspect, take more steps forward, and so on, until you reach your goal. Notice, problem-solving is tested in action, not just in your mind, and after testing, you'll often gain more insights and knowledge that you can then use to generate more solutions, eventually leading you to the solution you were looking for all along. Too often people sit at home speculating and wasting days, weeks or even years of their life. Don't be one of them. Go out and have experiences, because they help us to learn and move forward much faster than only speculating from the sidelines.

Now, let's take a look at the first three simple solution-finding strategies – good questions, brainstorming and physical movement – to help you on your way. As we explore them, bear the following in mind.

Asking yourself good questions is a strategy that you should use every time you think about how you're going to solve your challenges, whether in your mind or on paper. Asking good questions will, therefore, come into use when using the other two problem-solving strategies: brainstorming and physical movement.

Plus, you can do these three in any order and some of them together. You might use brainstorming and then physical movement to further develop the ideas generated during your brainstorming session, or you might use physical movement and then have a brainstorming session using the insights gained during the physical movement period, or you might use good questions and physical movement together.

Equally, you might ask yourself (and answer) a list of good questions on paper, then brainstorm some key ideas that seem to be flowing for you as a result of your question-and-answer session, and then use physical movement to further generate ideas and/or reach decisions on solutions you are going to test.

Asking Good Questions

We have to give our brain permission to search for, and find, answers. This permission comes in the form we talk to ourselves. If we talk to ourselves in statements, we are telling our brain that we have made our mind up and the topic isn't open for discussion or exploration. However, if we ask our brain a question, we are telling our brain to go and search for the answer. If we keep asking our brain the same question in different ways, or simply lots of different questions, and allow all answers to come without fear of negative judgement from ourselves, then like a good servant, the brain will respond and present the answers it has found in due course.

Here's the thing, though: any old question will not do. How you phrase the question will determine what sort of answer you get and will also influence your emotions positively or negatively.

We've looked at the power of thoughts and the importance of a self-serving positive outlook on challenges (Resilience Pillar 1) but now you'll notice what a difference they make to your problem-solving approach (Resilience Pillar 3). Let's assume Rebecca is having marital problems and arguments seem to be regular occurrences which are on the rise. Rebecca is desperate to fix her marital problems (Resilience Pillar 2) and so starts trying to solve the problems (Resilience Pillar 3) with the use of one of these two questions. The first is problem-focused and disempowering; the second is solution-focused and empowering:

◊ 'Why is it that, whatever I say, he always misunderstands me and we always end up arguing?'

◊ 'How can I communicate differently so that my husband understands what I am trying to say, and we have a relaxed discussion about it?'

Problem-focused questions focus the mind on the problem. Solution-focused questions focus the mind on the possible solutions.

Empowering questions highlight that we have responsibility over our own lives, and they nurture our well-being and make us proactive. Disempowering questions suggest that we lack control of our own lives, hindering our well-being and making us inactive.

Your resilience-o-meter will tell you if you are asking yourself a solution-focused, empowering question or a problem-focused, disempowering question. The former will make you feel lighter and more relaxed; the latter will make you feel heavier and more tense. Your mind will also tell you which one you're asking: the former will make you feel in control and optimistic; the latter will make you feel somewhat helpless and pessimistic.

So asking yourself solution-focused, empowering questions is vital, for it gives your brain permission to search for answers to your problems. Remember also that negative words can put you into fight-or-flight mode in less than a second. Therefore, minimising the use of negative words and focusing on solutions and empowerment will help you to positively regulate your emotions, which is important for resilience.

Focus on one challenge at a time. If you have multiple challenges that you need to problem-solve, start with your priority, the one that feels most important for you to make progress on first. It's better to make reasonable progress on one issue and then bring other challenges into focus as you create the head space and resilience to deal with them too.

Use questions that start with who, what, when, where, why and how to help you to think about solutions. For example:

◊ Who might be able to give me some moral support?
◊ What benefits will I reap from overcoming this obstacle?
◊ When do I need to have solved this problem by?
◊ Where can I get more information to help me learn about this topic?
◊ Why do these types of situations scare me?
◊ How can I start to improve my overall confidence in simple ways, day-to-day?

You can either ask questions in your mind or on a piece of paper (the latter is better if you have the opportunity to do it), either as a series of questions or one main question to be answered in order for you to overcome the challenge. This brings us nicely onto brainstorming, which can help you either answer the questions you've been asking or generate more ideas related to the questions or answers you've been exploring.

Brainstorming

Brainstorming is great because it really lends itself to creative problem-solving in a number of ways. It enables us to start with a blank sheet of paper, persuading us to start afresh with no prior agenda.

You can then place in the middle of that sheet of paper (or wherever it pleases you), either (a) the overarching, empowering, solution-focused question you are trying to answer in order to overcome your challenge, or (b) keywords for generating ideas. For example:

◇ What could I do to help me build my confidence in easy ways?

◇ How can I get more people buying my company's products?

◇ How can (spouse's name) and I get the excitement back in our marriage?

Or:

◇ Confidence-building

◇ Successful promoting/selling products

◇ Exciting marriage

If you add ideas and inspiration to the page, it usually helps you to form long-term memories from them and means you don't have to worry about forgetting them, as you have a written record; thereby conserving more energy and focus for creative problem-solving.

Get additional ideas and help from the internet, library, shops, local services, professionals, loved ones and any other places or people happy to help.

When we are thinking creatively and writing our ideas down, we must not judge our ideas; we must simply catch all of them. Alex Osborn, a high-flying advertising executive who wrote an influential book on creative problem-solving in the mid-twentieth century, suggested that an environment in which all ideas are welcomed and no ideas are judged results in significantly better ideas-generation, and ultimately leads to solving problems.[84]

Most creative problem-solving is a work-in-progress and you can easily make it so by leaving the brainstorming paper somewhere easily accessible with a pen nearby, so that as and when you have epiphanies, you can add them to the page. On and off you will add more ideas and more solutions as you consciously and subconsciously mull them over whilst honouring Resilience Pillar 3 (a problem-solving approach).

To complement asking good questions and brainstorming strategies, movement is important.

Physical Movement

It's amazing how quickly our brain starts to generate ideas when we get up from where we have been sitting for some time and go for a walk, all the while still searching for inspiration and answers. Movement in the body somehow creates movement in the mind. It makes being more reflective and introspective so much easier and it makes the process move along much more quickly.

Have you ever noticed how differently conversations can flow when you're out walking with someone, or how many good ideas and epiphanies you can have when you're on a treadmill or taking a stroll in the park? Well, as it happens, walking improves 'divergent thinking' – the use of creative thinking to generate ideas – so it's a good idea to walk when you want to problem-solve.[85]

Researchers at Stanford University tested different conditions for creative thinking: (a) sitting indoors, (b) walking indoors on a treadmill facing a blank wall, (c) walking outdoors in the built-up university campus, and (d) being rolled along in a wheelchair outdoors on campus. In some experiments, participants were made to walk and then sit or sit and then walk or sit twice but in two different rooms (for a change of scenery). No matter the environmental conditions, the results were clear. The physical state of walking, whether indoors on a treadmill facing a blank wall, or outdoors amongst buildings (not nature), significantly improved participants' creativity. What's more, walking and then sitting also produced significant effects on participants' creativity, demonstrating that walking has a residual effect on creative thinking, even once a person has sat down and some time has elapsed. In the three relevant experiments conducted, 81 per cent, 88 per cent and 100 per cent of participants were more creative when walking than when sitting. The message is pretty clear: when you need to problem-solve creatively, walking can substantially enhance creativity.

Warning: you may strain muscles as you excitedly log your ideas into your phone, but it might just be worth it!

Even if we scale this down significantly, have you ever noticed how just getting up and moving around for a few moments can change your perspective, renew your energy, create greater clarity and sometimes generate new answers and epiphanies? When you're stuck in a mental rut, try moving to a different part of the room and sitting or standing in a different direction, or moving to a different part of the building altogether. Sometimes we just need a little movement or a change of scenery for a change of emotions and insights.

Manipulating Your Perspective

Angling the lens of our mind elsewhere enables us to view things differently, and this can help us to generate new thoughts and ideas. Sometimes, it also helps to pretend we're someone else solving the problem. For example:

◊ 'What advice would I give my best friend if they were in my position?'
◊ 'What would my dad advise me to do?'

Other times when we feel 'too close to the problem', it helps to look at things through our own eyes but with an out-of-body type of experience, so that we can take a step back or rise above the predicament. This can help us to feel immediately calmer when we're panicking, and to think more clearly when things seem cloudy, giving us a broader picture. We can force this sort of out-of-body experience by changing our time perspective, even when the task itself has nothing to do with 'time', and by doing so we can enhance our insights and abstract creativity.[86] For example, you can imagine your life a year later and/or imagine working on the task in hand a year later to gain perspective and, subsequently, increase how many creative ideas or solutions you generate.

Interestingly, whilst the distant-time perspective can help 'divergent thinking' to generate creative ideas, it can actually hinder 'convergent thinking' – the use of logical thinking to create executable action steps to move us to our end goal. So, if you are going to play around with time to help you with the three afore-mentioned strategies – good questions, brainstorming and physical movement – you should:

◊ think from a distant-time perspective to help creative problem-solving when abstract thinking is required and you want to generate ideas;
◊ think from a current or near-future time perspective when more concrete thinking is needed to allow you to be analytical, logical and organise ideas into a flow of action.

Once you know which perspective to use depending on the type of problem you're trying to solve, you can ask yourself a question to help you tap into either one, e.g.:

◊ Distant-time perspective: 'What advice would I give my younger self if I were ten years older, looking back at myself as I am now?'
◊ Current or near-future time perspective: 'What's the best way to execute this plan right now?'

Daydreaming is Good for You

Lastly, be sure to embrace daydreaming. It's not just for kids; it's especially important for adults, too. You may have been told off in school for daydreaming but research suggests it helps us to achieve our important goals. When we are daydreaming, we are actually engaging more of our brain than previously thought. We now see that in addition to using the brain's 'default network', which handles easy, routine tasks, the brain's 'executive network', which handles complex problem-solving, also becomes activated.[87] It appears that when we are daydreaming, we may be subconsciously problem-solving the bigger puzzles in our life, even though we may not be paying full attention to the task in hand.

To make the most of this, you can purposefully induce daydreaming by focusing on a simple task and then allowing your brain to wander; for example, having a shower, cleaning the home, playing a computer game or connecting the pieces of a jigsaw puzzle.

Factors that Affect our Problem-Solving Ability

I love that psychology, neuroscience and other such disciplines that teach us how the human brain and body function offer us insights into how just the slightest tweak of some sort can create welcome results. This is how you're able to build your resilience in just four weeks.

Problem-solving is one such area in which we can tweak our thoughts and behaviours in order to achieve a different outcome, just as we can change our emotions with simple tricks. Here are some additional cool insights for you to use to your problem-solving advantage.

Mixing it up

How often do you mix up your routine? If you're in a mental rut, chances are you have the same routine most days. It can be so easy to fall into routines (habits) but once you're aware, it can also be easy to schedule some plans into your diary to change your routine by trying one new thing a week, big or small, e.g.:

◊ a new restaurant or cooking a different meal at home,
◊ a new park for walks or a new place for you and friends to talk,
◊ driving to work in a different direction or shopping in a different store,
◊ a dance class or art class, or some other activity you've never done before.

Never underestimate the power of small changes to your routine to eventually lead to big positive changes. I see it happen . . . a lot! I also see how completely closed off from common sense clients' minds can be when they are stuck in a routine. You've got to mix things up. Remember: something new in, something new out.

Positive emotions help

We know that negative emotions disrupt the brain's cognitive functions so always ensure you're in a positive emotional state when you're about to spend a considerable amount of time problem-solving. Enhance your problem-solving ability by purposefully inducing positive emotions.[88] For example, do something to put yourself into a positive mood using tips from the chapter on emotions – like watching a funny video for a few minutes or talking to someone who uplifts your mood – before you sit down to generate ideas or go for a 'creative walk'.

Sleep deprivation hinders

Earlier we learnt that the brain needs sleep to consolidate memories and gain perspective on stressful events (see page 136). The brain also benefits from sleep when solving problems. In one study, participants were set tasks in which they were expected to respond quicker over time as they learnt sequence responses. Unbeknown to them during training, there was a hidden rule underlying all sequences that would enable them to significantly increase their task completion speed much quicker than they would purely through practising the sequence responses. The initial task training was followed by either eight hours of overnight sleep, staying awake overnight or staying awake during the day, and then participants were retested. More than twice as many participants who slept for eight hours, as opposed to those who didn't, gained insight into that hidden rule that helped them to complete the tasks much quicker than they could have otherwise.[89] It's possible that our brain restructures memories during sleep, helping us to gain new insights from the same information. You will have experienced this yourself at some point – struggling hard to solve a problem all day only to find that the answer effortlessly popped into your head the following day after you had slept well.

Although convergent (linear) thinking tends to be more resilient to short-term sleep deprivation, divergent (creative) thinking can be hindered by just one night's sleep loss.[90] Clearly, sleep is incredibly important to resilience as we need our creative abilities to overcome the challenges in our path. Therefore, sleep strengthens Resilience Pillar 3 whilst even one night of sleep loss weakens it.

Be sure to get a good night's sleep, even when you feel as if you're pushed for time because you have to hit a tight deadline. Be sure to do something to help you to de-stress if you're struggling with insomnia due to worries about your challenges and goals. Sometimes it can help to write stuff down before bed as then you give your brain permission to let go. Sometimes it helps to tire your brain and body out with something like physical exercise or reading a book. Other times doing something to help you relax can work, like having a hot shower, taking a soak in the bath or drinking hot milk before bedtime.

You can even upgrade the system when you hit the recharge button. When you're feeling optimistic at bedtime, think hard for a minute or two about any problems you want to solve the next day or at any time (even write it down, e.g. 'I want to work out how to . . .'), and with your self-talk, tell your brain to go and find the answer! Let it work on your problems and goals whilst you enjoy your sleep!

⊨ OVER TO YOU ⊨

Rewire Your Brain for Resilience in Four Weeks or Less

You now have the tools at your disposal to create the new resilient you in four weeks, and to sustain it thereafter for the rest of your life.

To rewire your brain for a resilience habit, meet every challenge you encounter from this point on with an immediate positive outlook on challenges (Resilience Pillar 1) closely followed by a problem-solving approach (Resilience Pillar 3).

1. Notice challenge
2. Positive outlook
3. Problem-solve

Put your positive outlook on challenges (Resilience Pillar 1) into your own words that you can repeat over and over; something that makes you feel empowered, optimistic and confident, e.g. 'Challenges guide me towards my goals and happiness' or 'Every challenge helps me in some way'. Write it down now and memorise it in the next forty-eight hours.

By the end of the four weeks, resilience will be second nature for you and this will be your new 'normal'. Thereafter, you'll continue facing challenges in this way and using the resilience-strengthening exercises in this book to reinforce your resilience every time it becomes eroded and weakened.

Tips on how to Skilfully and Easily Employ Resilience Pillar 3 – A Problem-Solving Approach

Do this task now, and then continue daily or every other day, as described below, during your four-week resilience plan. Do steps one to three together, every time, immediately after one another.

1. Take a resilience reading using your resilience-o-meter.
   Pinpoint its level on your body and make a written note
   of it along with the date and time.
2. Write down an obstacle that you need to problem-solve
   in order to achieve important goals, big or small. (Just
   focus on one to begin with; bring in more as you create
   the head space and resilience to deal with another
   challenge.)
3. Every day or every two days, starting today, spend five to
   thirty minutes (or longer) problem-solving these obstacles. The more motivated and resilient you're feeling, the
   more you'll do and the more often. Remember, you'll do
   a lot of this problem-solving in your head as you're going
   about the rest of your day-to-day life, pausing only to
   make notes as required.

Today and every subsequent day, use the following techniques:

- Ask yourself goal-focused, solution-focused, empowering
  questions that start with who, what, when, where, why
  and how.
- Brainstorm your answers and any other notable thoughts
  you have, with pen and paper. Welcome and capture all
  ideas.
- Further explore the thoughts and ideas that stand out as
  the best and most likely to be useful. Ask yourself further
  questions, or brainstorm further on new sheets of paper,
  for each of these.
- Use physical movement to get your creative juices
  flowing.
- Use others' perspectives and distant-time perspectives for
  generating creative ideas and possible solutions.
- Practise activities that help to induce daydreaming.

Treat all problem-solving as a work-in-progress and keep your brainstorming papers somewhere accessible with a pen by them at all times so you can add to them as you go. Feel free to do more than thirty minutes' problem-solving at any one time.

Persistence is vital and pays off when you keep asking good questions and keep searching for answers, sometimes consciously, other times subconsciously. The more time you spend thinking consciously about your goals and any challenges to overcome, the more time your subconscious mind will spend thinking about them.

Importantly, each time you make progress on the problem-solving, take another resilience-o-meter reading, noting the level, the date and the time.

Watch your resilience (reading) go up as you problem-solve further and further until you actually solve the challenges to the point of achieving your end goals.

SUMMARY

Clearly and specifically programme your brain's problem-solving 'sat-nav' with the problem (starting position) and the goal (end destination), and then search until you find the answer consciously or it comes to you from your subconscious.

Use good questions, brainstorming with pen and paper, walking and movement, altering perspectives and daydreaming to help generate ideas and epiphanies, and use positive emotions and a good night's sleep to further enhance your problem-solving ability.

Most of all, keep faith. It will happen. You will get your answers if you search relentlessly until you do.

Intuitive Decision-Making

'Intuition is the clear conception of the whole at once.'
Johann Kaspar Lavater

We've been looking at how to make the most of conscious problem-solving strategies and how the subconscious mind then continues working as a result of your conscious efforts. Since making great decisions is critical to successfully problem-solving challenges (Resilience Pillar 3), I'll leave you with one last lesson before you start your four-week resilience plan. You should use your intuition to help you make great decisions.

Research demonstrates that our subconscious mind makes decisions before we consciously become aware of those decisions and then 'consciously make' those same decisions![91] Clearly there's much more to decision-making than just thinking. There is stuff going on 'under the bonnet' that we're not privy to which helps us to make good decisions, but intuition can give us a sneak peek.

Intuition is your ability to understand or know something instinctively, without conscious reasoning. It allows you to access information known subconsciously by your brain and body that you don't yet know consciously. This additional information will help you make great decisions.

Your intuition serves up information, and answers, that are often quicker and more accurate than your conscious reasoning can provide. For this reason your intuition can be an invaluable tool when you (a) have to act fast, (b) have to make a decision with little information, and/or (c) are simply struggling to make a conscious final decision one way or the other.

We usually make intuitive decisions based on a feeling. Initially, we don't consciously know the reason for the feeling; we just know that something felt good or felt bad, or felt right or felt wrong. This occurs because the brain uses past experiences and new information coming through the senses to make a decision subconsciously.[92] This happens so quickly that we can sometimes only sense the aftermath: the feeling. Later, sometimes hours or even weeks later, our conscious mind tends to catch up, enabling us to identify specifically why we had experienced that good feeling or bad feeling. In other words, **your body physically reacts to information and you can tune in to that bodily reaction, even when you don't yet know what specifically it's reacting to**. By doing so, you can use your body as a conduit of that subconscious wisdom and use your bodily reaction to help you make great decisions, and quickly.

Trusting your gut feeling can help you to tap into information and answers that will help you almost instantaneously! That is incredible: a highly self-serving function of the human body that you should be using just as you use your eyes to see and your ears to hear. Remember, the brain runs and manages far more processes subconsciously than it does consciously, and we see this in our minute-to-minute existence. We don't think about which muscles we need to engage to walk, for example; the brain does this subconsciously.

You Know, Even When You Think You Don't

You've probably used your intuition at some point in your life and consequently made great choices, even though you may not have identified it as intuition.

Imagine what you could achieve if you could know things before others, and before you would expect yourself to . . .

It's surprising how much you can begin to 'guess' correctly when you use your intuition. Sometimes that means trusting the changing sensations inside your body, but other times it's about trusting that voice in your head that seems to answer before you've had time to consciously or thoughtfully evaluate your options or your bodily sensations. That is how quickly your intuition can work.

Many people are intuitive but abandon their intuition and consequently make so many poor choices that they end up off-track from their goals and feeling miserable. This often comes back to statements from our upbringing: 'Trust your head, not your heart', 'Women are emotional', 'Men are rational', and all that nonsense we've been fed that makes us feel that we're being unrealistic and fanciful if we trust something other than our 'analytical head' to make decisions. The funny thing is, when someone answers from their heart rather than their head, their facial muscles tend to be much more relaxed. That's a physical sign right there that one form of finding an answer is effortless and one is – well – not. And it's not about how serene you look when you answer using your intuition; it's about what that can do for your life and mental well-being. The inner peace and good fortune that come from allowing your intuition to help you make great decisions, effortlessly, all the time, I can't even begin to do justice to; you'll find out for yourself.

We've been taught for years that we should use our head rather than our heart when making decisions, but is it even sound advice? We now know that the heart is not just a blood pump but actually a source of intelligence with its own independent complex nervous system, known as the 'heart-brain'.[93] The heart makes many of its own decisions independently of the brain, and is in a constant two-way dialogue with the brain.

The heart also produces an electromagnetic field that is about sixty times stronger than the brain's, as measured by an electrocardiogram (ECG). This powerful electromagnetic field can be detected and measured up to several feet away from a person's body and, when people touch or are in proximity to each other, there can be a transference of electromagnetic energy.[94] For example, researchers have noticed that the electromagnetic energy from one person's heart can register in the other person's brain activity and on their body surfaces, such as their legs and forearms. So our bodies are immersed in and sensing electromagnetic energy from other people. That's interesting because we often hear people say they 'got a certain vibe' from someone or 'picked up on someone's energy'. Given that information about our emotional state is encoded in our heart's electromagnetic field,[95] perhaps that transfer of electromagnetic energy carries useful information to us about other people to help us suss them out or make decisions.

Sometimes we just know things, and we know them so quickly that it's like putting a search term into an internet search engine and getting an immediate answer. This is partially because we absorb way more information through all of our senses than we consciously realise we are at the time. So keep an open mind about what you think you know. You often know a lot more than you think you do. Plus, subconsciously stored information your intuition accesses can also be stored more accurately and be more accessible than information stored consciously. In one study, for example, participants were asked to memorise information they would later be asked to recall. Some were distracted during the memorising task whilst some were not. Those who were distracted whilst memorising the information later recalled the correct information, even though consciously they felt they were making a guess and couldn't actually remember the information.[96] In fact, the 'distracted' participants who guessed their answers were more accurate than the 'undistracted' participants who 'knew' their answers! So we notice more and calculate more than we think we do, and we just have to take that sneak peek under the bonnet when we want to. Before we look at intuition in more detail, let me show you how simple and easy it is for you to start accessing your intuition from today.

⊨ OVER TO YOU ⊨

When you want to decipher which decision is right for you, whether you have multiple options to choose from or a relationship to pursue or distance yourself from, use the upcoming tips to help you tune in to your intuition and make great decisions quickly and easily.

Do what it takes to relax yourself and quiet your mind of distractions, as it's usually difficult to tune in to your intuition when you are not relaxed. A **quick pick-me-up** or **soothe-me session** to ease waves and storms and calm internal waters, at least temporarily, will help you to create the conditions necessary for accurately tuning in to your intuition. For example, lighting some candles, going for a brisk walk, taking a hot soak in the bath, having a positive word with yourself, or one of the other emotion-regulation strategies or self-care strategies we have discussed.

Focus your heart and mind on the thing you want answers about so you can tune in to the feeling, or perhaps the energy. Think of it like focusing your eyesight on something far away or listening out closely for something.

Very often it's the first answer that pops into your head before you've had time to consciously over-think it or even finish asking yourself the question! The answer rapidly flashes through your mind and feels detached from your conscious evaluating process.

Use bodily sensations or **physical signs** to establish how you feel about each possible option. For example, let's assume you need to make a decision and you have three options to choose from, 'X', 'Y' and 'Z':

- Imagine yourself pursuing one of the three possible options.
- As you wholeheartedly imagine pursuing that option, pay attention to the sensations you feel within your body and any involuntary body movements you notice.
- Repeat this exercise for each of the three options.
- You'll usually find that one of the options triggers the most relaxed feeling or physical state compared with the other options, as you vividly imagine each one separately. The presence of a relaxed state is a good indicator as to which decision may be the right one for you. The presence of tension is a good sign that something may not be right for you.
- The internal bodily sensations may be felt around your chest, back, neck, shoulders, scalp, stomach or elsewhere. Your most obvious telltale sign regions will be specific to you. Certainly, though, the heart area is a useful one to tune in to as you can sometimes detect beat-to-beat changes, and general tension and relaxation, which can help signpost you towards the right decision.
- The external physical indicators might be involuntary body movements like clenching your fist, shaking your leg, tapping your feet or rubbing your head, which might represent anxiety about the option that you are considering in that moment.
- Consider the physiological and/or physical response as your subconscious mind's way of telling you, 'I've scanned all the information, stored and new, and I suggest this option is safe or right for you and that option is unsafe or wrong for you.' When you have the courage to follow your gut feeling, watch how hours, days or weeks later, your conscious mind delivers the specific reasons that support your intuitive hunch.

Monitor your results to build your self-belief, even if you don't always have the courage to follow your gut feeling (your intuition). To do this, regardless of whether you follow through on your intuitive hunch, use any opportunity you can to make an intuitive decision about something important, like whether to date someone or go to an event, or intuitively guess something silly like how much the supermarket shopping is going to cost or how many grapes are in the bowl. As you monitor the outcomes after some minutes or weeks have passed – whichever time period might be necessary – you'll hone your skill and increase your confidence.

Use common sense when applying these tips. If you're feeling tense about something, use conscious reasoning and questions to decipher if the tension is due to your anxiety about doing something new (e.g. public speaking) or due to the option being fraught with problems (e.g. you don't have enough time to prepare and do well).

Your Skin Knows Way Before You Do

The human brain and body are so sophisticated it's mind-blowing. You're transmitting electromagnetic energy from your brain and heart, separately, and others are doing the same. Your skin also momentarily conducts electricity better when you react to something physiologically arousing in your internal body or external environment. The skin, it seems, does a lot of sensing and may be responsible for some of the symptomatic bodily sensations we access when we tune in to our intuition.

In one study, experiments were conducted on healthy individuals with 'normal' brain function and on patients with prefrontal damage in the brain (the front part located behind the forehead implicated in reasoning, decision making and more) as well as decision-making defects.[97] The participants' skin-conductance responses, decisions and awareness were all monitored throughout an experimental gambling game. For each round in the game, the participants were asked to choose a deck to draw a card from, with the goal of winning the most money during the game. The participants were presented with four decks of cards but unbeknown to them, two decks provided big wins followed by big losses whilst the other two safer decks provided small wins with only an occasional loss.

There were stark differences between the skin's physiological response and the conscious reasoning brain in the 'normal' participants. After choosing about ten cards their skin began to react (conduct electricity better) to the two high-risk decks, yet by card twenty they had all indicated that they were still completely unaware of any differences between the decks. At around card fifty, all the 'normal' participants began to guess that two of the decks were riskier and they continued to generate anticipatory skin-conductance responses whenever they considered choosing from the high-risk decks. It took roughly eighty cards for most of the 'normal' participants to consciously identify and articulate why the two high-risk decks were disadvantageous for the aim of the game and why the other two decks were advantageous.

Fascinatingly, the three 'normal' participants who did not consciously recognise the differences between the decks still made advantageous choices. Just as remarkably, the three patients with prefrontal brain damage who eventually recognised which decks were good for them and which were bad still continued to choose from the disadvantageous decks. These patients didn't display anticipatory skin-conductance, either.

It appears the brain relies on the body to help it make decisions, using the involuntary signals it receives from the body without our conscious awareness that this signalling is going on. Our bodies notice things quickly but it takes us quite a bit longer to consciously work the same things out in our brain such that we can express them. Plus, even when we haven't consciously worked stuff out we can still make better choices because our body steers our brain's decisions and our behaviours. Cheers, body–brain connection! If that's us on auto-pilot, imagine what we can do when we actually try to tune in to the body and its changing sensations.

This study also suggests that healthy people access records shaped by previous personal experiences of reward, punishment and their accompanying emotional states, and that damage to ventromedial cortices (part of the prefrontal cortex) prohibits access to some form of record of previous and related personal experience. So accessing subconsciously stored information is clearly important to intuition.

As in the card gambling experiment, other researchers have also found that the skin can react in response to emotionally arousing information it is absorbing subconsciously, this time visually.[98] In this study, images that would help them to answer a question were flashed for less than half a second in front of participants' eyes, fast enough for the participants to not be consciously aware of having seen them. Similarly, even without conscious awareness of the visual information, decision-making still improved as a result. Intuition also improved over time, suggesting practice helps us to improve our intuitive skills.[99]

Brace Yourself: It's About to Get Sci-Fi-Like!

What's intriguing is, even in instances where there is no prior knowledge based on memories or pattern-identification, our heart and skin still seem to sense things that are yet to unfold. How trippy and science-fiction-like is that! For example, in one study, participants were presented with a random selection of emotionally arousing and emotionally calm images on a screen. The participants' heart rates decelerated significantly more before a randomly selected, emotionally arousing image was shown compared to a randomly selected, emotionally calm image.[100]

Their hearts knew something they 'couldn't' have possibly known yet – but these findings have been replicated elsewhere, demonstrating what some researchers have termed 'intuitive foreknowledge' as noted by bodily measures, especially changes in the heart rhythm.[101] In another study, using skin-conductance and heart-rate variability (HRV) for detecting changes, a significant bodily response to as yet unknown knowledge in a roulette-type game began at around eighteen seconds prior to participants discovering the outcome of their bet.[102]

So to summarise, our bodies can quickly identify patterns that can help us to know which decisions are right for us, sometimes using this information in tandem with stored memories. The brain then subconsciously influences our decisions without our conscious awareness by using these bodily changes as a source of wisdom, as we saw in, amongst others, the card gambling experiment. A transference of energy can occur from human hearts to human brains and bodies, and the body also predicts the future somehow, so we now have an important channel of information: the body. In other words, your brain and body rapidly detect subtle information from the environment, and you can harness that power and improve it over time like any other skill.

Just one last thought to leave you with as you marvel at how incredible your brain and body are and how much more you can use them to your advantage. Upon reviewing decades of research, one researcher proposed that perhaps repeat entrepreneurs use their intuitive heart to locate future opportunities and bring them into being by passionately focusing on those opportunities. And that they do this by using their heart to detect energetic information about events that are yet to unfold in time and space, which cannot be based on stored memories (i.e. they use 'non-local intuition').[103]

Can we make our motivated desires happen with our heart and mind, with focus and intent? Maybe. One thing's for sure: the heart is a powerful, intelligent, independent sensory organ and so it's particularly useful to focus your mind on your heart area when you are tapping in to your intuition. Doing so will help you to detect your heart's beat-to-beat changes – your heart-rate variability (HRV) – which, importantly, is influenced by your emotions and so can give rapid insights. [104]

There is clearly another form of communication in our world that is unseen and unheard, and the heart is implicated. We can use our heart as a source of wisdom to help us make good decisions, keep us safe, have positive relationships and help ourselves to overcome challenges and achieve our goals.

Use Your Intuition

Like listening to a musician playing notes, when you focus your mind on your heart area, you can feel those beating notes playing. Whenever you need to make a decision, turn your attention inwards and use your intuition. Intuition helps keep you safe and moving in the direction of your goals quickly and easily. We've been talking about turning your attention inwards to your bodily sensations to help you gauge your current resilience level and the effects of your own thoughts; now you can use your bodily sensations to also figure out what else your body is sensing and reacting to.

The ability to rely on yourself for making great decisions at all times with help from your intuition reinforces your resilience armour because self-reliance is vital for resilience and underpins the Three Pillars of Resilience: a positive outlook on challenges, a driving motivation to achieve the end goal, and a problem-solving approach. Intuition also helps you to quickly discover which goals are your true goals and which are not so that you don't waste your life focusing on and worrying about the things that really aren't important to you. Plus, of course, a problem-solving approach (Resilience Pillar 3) requires good decisions and your intuition can help you massively.

Remember, your subconscious mind can know why you got an intuitive sense about someone or something, drawing you towards one decision over another, days or even weeks before your conscious mind does. So by tuning in to responses from, or changes in, the bodily sensations we sense within us, we can near-instantly know which people, goals, situations and decisions are right for us.

Intuition is incredibly fun to use and you can definitely hone it with repetition, so start using it today on any little thing you can, so that you can build the skill quickly and, at the same time, your resilience armour.

By using your intuition, you can make rapid decisions – life-changing and life-saving decisions – and you can make great decisions effortlessly at any time. Intuition serves your goals, happiness, life purpose and survival.

SUMMARY

Our subconscious mind often notices information and makes decisions before the conscious mind is aware of that very same information and those decisions. If we can attune to the physiological changes within us, we can use them to signpost us towards good decisions far sooner than if we wait for conscious awareness of the same information.

Intuition seems to work by accessing information captured and stored both consciously and subconsciously. However, instances of intuition about the future where there is no prior knowledge in the form of memories or pattern-identification also exist. Pretty incredible!

Once you start using your intuition successfully, you'll think not using it is a major handicap.

Part 3:

The Resilient Me Four-Week Plan and Troubleshooting

Four Weeks to a Resilient Me

'Repetition of the same thought or physical action develops into a habit which, repeated frequently enough, becomes an automatic reflex.' Norman Vincent Peale

So that's it, Winner! All you now need to do to become resilient in four weeks is spend the time indulging self-serving choices.

As you will have noticed, creating the newly refined version of yourself – resilient you – isn't so much about the challenges you are facing as it is about (a) how you use your thoughts and behaviours to *respond* to those challenges the very moment you encounter them and (b) how you maintain positive, self-serving habits every day to help you.

Remember that resilience requires:

a. The Three Pillars of Resilience be present, i.e. you have: (i) a positive outlook on challenges; (ii) a driving motivation to achieve an end goal; (iii) a problem-solving approach.

b. That you train your brain to create a habit of responding to all challenges resiliently, with that three step process: (i) notice the challenge; (ii) immediately affirm a positive outlook on the challenge, (iii) immediately begin problem-solving to eventually overcome the challenge.

c. That you use the eight simple resilience strengthening habits covered in the previous chapters to help you easily honour the three pillars, and quickly train your brain for a resilience habit:

1. *Create* self-serving, positive thoughts.
2. Regulate your emotions with intention.
3. Build and nurture positive relationships.
4. Indulge proper self-care.
5. Close unpleasant chapters.
6. Set achievable 'true goals'.
7. Use problem-solving thoughts and behaviours.
8. Use intuition to make great decisions.

You might find the simple three-step process for rewiring your brain ('b' above) is sufficient for creating the resilient you in four weeks. On the other hand, if any of the above eight resilience strengthening habits is missing or underdeveloped, you will need to carry out a few simple additional activities during your four-week plan. For example, you might need to socialise with loved ones more to help maintain positive emotions, indulge a bit more pampering to help you feel valuable and deserving of happiness, go for a brisk walk to help alleviate anxiety or low moods, or use affirmations to create self-serving thoughts throughout the day or to build self-belief to achieve goals.

Now you'll need to spend between ten and thirty minutes (or more if need be) to create your personalised four-week plan so that the advice in this book is tailored to *your specific needs*.

Create Your Personalised Four-Week Plan

Below you are signposted to the detailed 'Over To You' exercises that will help you to quickly and easily retrain yourself for resilience during your four-week plan. **Some exercises won't be relevant to you:** if you already achieve the 'Your objective' statement, just skip to the next one in the list.

Remember, we are a product of our habits and anything we do often enough becomes a habit because, through repetition, the brain learns how to execute that habit well and with ease as you create 'well-travelled' neural pathways. Over time, the brain conserves energy by automating habits and we experience that as something 'feeling easy to do'. Where you are right now is the product of your habits to date. Where you will be at the end of your four-week plan will be shaped by the habits you indulge in that time period. Use the signposted 'Over To You' exercises below to create your personalised four-week plan and **schedule ongoing activities into a four-week planner**. You will find it helpful to *also* **create a to-do list of the one-off activities** you need to do on your first day or within your first few days (as per the instructions below). This way you can easily do all the one-off and ongoing activities you need to do to become the cool, calm, collected resilient you during your four-week plan.

Examples of SMART goals are in the 'Over To You' exercise on page 126. Overleaf, there's an example of week one of a personalised planner to help you visualise yours. In the proceeding weeks you might move things around, add goals, and increase or decrease the frequency and length of activities.

	Mon	Tue	Wed
Week 1	Eat well 24/7	Eat well 24/7	Eat well 24/7
	Positive thoughts & emotions 24/7	Positive thoughts & emotions 24/7	Positive thoughts & emotions 24/7
	30 mins brisk walk 5:30–6 p.m.	Problem-solving session 12–12:30 p.m.	30 mins brisk walk 5–5:30 p.m.
	Meditation 6–6:15 p.m.	Me-time 5–5:30 p.m.	Me-time 8–9 p.m.
	Problem-solving session 6:30–7 p.m.	Hobby 'X' 7–9 p.m.	Meditation 9–9:30 p.m.
	Me-time 8–9 p.m.	Quality time with spouse 9-30–11:30 p.m.	Quality time with spouse 9:30–10 p.m.
	Quality time with spouse 9–10 p.m.	Good sleep 12–8 a.m.	Good sleep 12–8 a.m.
	Good sleep 12–8 a.m.		
Week 2			
Week 3			
Week 4			

Resilience Strengthening Habit 1:
Create self-serving, positive thoughts

Change self-sabotaging attitudes (filters)
Your objective: To only hold self-serving attitudes.
Dose: Do this on day one of your four-week plan.
How to: Use the 'Over To You' exercises on pages 48 and 51

Understand the impact of your negative thoughts
Your objective: To be averse to sabotaging yourself with negative thoughts.

Thu	Fri	Sat	Sun
Eat well 24/7	Eat well 24/7	Eat well 24/7	Eat well 24/7
Positive thoughts & emotions 24/7	Positive thoughts & emotions 24/7	Positive thoughts & emotions 24/7	Positive thoughts & emotions 24/7
Problem-solving session 5–5:30 p.m.	30 mins brisk walk 5:30–6 p.m.	Meditation 10–10:30 a.m.	See family 11 a.m.–2 p.m.
Me-time 8–9 p.m.	Me-time 6–6:30 p.m.	Problem-solving session 11:30 a.m.–12 p.m.	Me-time (incl. pampering) 3–5 p.m.
Quality time with spouse 9:30–10:30 p.m.	See a friend 8 p.m.+	Quality time with spouse 12–4 p.m.	Quality time with spouse 5–7 p.m.
Good sleep 12–8 a.m.	Good sleep 2–9 a.m.	Me-time 8–9 p.m.	Good sleep 12–8 a.m.
		Good sleep 12–8 a.m.	

Dose: Do this on day one of your four-week plan.

How to: Use the 'Over To You' exercises on pages 59 and 66.

Minimise time spent worrying

Your objective: To create a habit of worrying little-to-zero of the time by wiring your brain for it.

Dose: 1–5 minute mini meditations as and when required or 10-30 minute long meditations 3–7 times per week if required.

How to: Use the 'Over To You' exercise on page 66.

Create self-serving habits and eliminate self-sabotaging habits

Your objective: To create good habits that will help you to achieve your goals and happiness, including a habit of resilience, and to eliminate bad habits that are pushing your goals and happiness further away, including a lack of resilience.

Dose: Daily, at every opportunity you get to change your brain's old habit and create your new preferred habit.

How to: Use the second part of the 'Over To You' exercise on page 72.

Only talk to yourself in positive words

Your objective: To use your self-talk to steer your life in a desirable direction, only.

Dose: Every second of every day.

How to: Use the 'Over To You' exercise on page 80.

Resilience Strengthening Habit 2: Regulate your emotions with intention

Make sense of negative emotions to become unstuck

Your objective: To quickly get yourself out of negative emotional ruts so you can problem-solve anything, including what needs to happen for you to feel good again.

Dose: As and when required.

How to: Use the 'Over To You' exercise on page 25.

Reappraise past memories that are holding you back

Your objective: To release the hold a significant past life event seems to have over your present that is also sabotaging your future.

Dose: Once on day one of your four-week plan. After your attempt on day one, if on day two or three you feel you need to reappraise the memory further do so again on those days but feel sure that you have successfully reappraised by day three, get someone to help you find alternative appraisals / perspectives if need be.

How to: Use the 'Over To You' exercise on page 90 to help you to reappraise it and release its hold for once and for all. Doing so will help you move towards your goals and overcome any challenges much more effortlessly without that feeling of self-doubt, self-loathing or low self-worth weighing you down.

Use sensory changes to help regulate your emotions

Your objective: To identify and use sensory changes to help transform your emotional state.

Dose: Make all permanent sensory changes during the first four days of your four-week plan and use the temporary changes as and when required.

How to: Use the 'Over To You' exercise on page 92.

Use long-term emotion regulation strategies

Your objective: To create your timetable of happiness-maintenance activities to help sustain fairly consistently positive emotions long-term.

Dose: Socialising one to two times per week; indulging interests or hobbies two to seven times per week; being spiritual weekly, daily or as desired; striving for and achieving goals daily or near daily.

How to: Use the 'Over To You' exercise on page 95.

Use quick 'pick-me-ups' to further help create positive emotions

Your objective: To maintain positive emotions throughout your four week plan and quickly take emotions from negative to positive with positivity boosts.

Dose: One per week of your four week plan.

How to: Use the 'Over To You' exercise on page 98.

Resilience Strengthening Habit 3:
Build and nurture positive relationships

Create and/or nurture positive relationships
Your objective: To maintain ongoing resilience with a network of positive relationships.
Dose: Daily and weekly.
How to: Use the 'Over To You' exercise on page 109.

Use giving to make yourself and others happy
Your objective: To use selflessness to help build self-worth and happiness.
Dose: At least once per week.
How to: Use the 'Over To You' exercise on page 116.

Get support from your significant others
Your objective: To ensure the important people in your life support your goals and your methods for achieving them.
Dose: Do this on day one of your four-week plan and then as and when required.
How to: Use the 'Over To You' exercise on page 117.

Make relationship choices and habits that positively shape your self-worth and self-esteem
Your objective: To surround yourself only with relationships that nourish your self-esteem and self-worth.
Dose: On day one of your four-week plan, make thoughtful choices about your existing relationships and then maintain good choices, daily. Get a loved one or professional to help you if need be.
How to: Use the 'Over To You' exercises on pages 124 and 127.

Resilience Strengthening Habit 4: Indulge proper self-care

Use self-compassion to be happy and to achieve goals

Your objective: To use self-compassionate thoughts and behaviours, only.

Dose: As and when required (i.e. whenever lacking self-compassion) but take a quick look now, too.

How to: Use the 'Over To You' exercise on page 132.

Use ongoing physical exercise for its many vital benefits for resilience

Your objective: To reap the benefits physical exercise has on your thoughts, emotions, mental well-being, resilience, problem-solving, learning and improving skills.

Dose: Three to five times a week for at least thirty minutes. Additionally, use as and when required for as long as required for problem-solving or for shifting the feeling of anxiety or tension from your body and relaxing your mind.

How to: Use the 'Over To You' exercise on page 134.

Use a proper night's sleep to remember, reappraise, recharge, reset

Your objective: To allow your body to perform its necessary functions for mental and physical health and well-being.

Dose: Daily.

How to: Use the 'Over To You' exercise on page 137.

Maintain cleanliness and nurture yourself with pampering

Your objective: To elevate your self-image and self-worth with proper cleanliness and self-love.

Dose: Maintain cleanliness daily. Pamper yourself as required.

How to: Use the 'Over To You' exercise on page 140.

Maintain proper nutrition for a fighting-fit body

Your objective: To eat tasty, healthy food and drink plenty of water, every day.

Dose: Daily. Plan a simple, healthy eating/drinking regime on day one of your four-week plan.

How to: Use the 'Over To You' exercise on page 142.

Use me-time for a recharge

Your objective: To take ownership of how much time and space you need to feel rested and resilient and ready for the world.

Dose: Daily. On day one, schedule this into your planner for your four-week plan.

How to: Use the 'Over To You' exercise on page 144.

Reduce information overload to increase time, energy and focus

Your objective: To recoup wasted energy where you can so that you can more easily feel resilient day-to-day and achieve your goals and happiness.

Dose: Daily. Plan simple, small, significant changes to your routine on day one of your four-week plan.

How to: Use the 'Over To You' exercise on page 147.

Resilience Strengthening Habit 5: Close unpleasant chapters

Get closure or draw a line under your past to move on

Your objective: To leave the past in the past so it stops sabotaging your present and your future.

Dose: Do this on day one or at least no later than day four of your four-week plan.

How to: Use the 'Over To You' exercise on page 153.

Resilience Strengthening Habit 6: Set achievable 'true goals'

Your goals and reason for picking up this book might be basic survival goals (like food, water, shelter, clothing or physical/

mental well-being) or important life goals or anything in between. Because Resilience Pillar 2 is a driving motivation to achieve the end goal, we need to know what that goal is. In the midst of a challenging moment you can ask yourself:

  i. What is the end goal? (e.g. To keep my job to pay the bills.)
  ii. Am I motivated to achieve it? (e.g. Yes!)
  iii. What might help me to achieve it? (e.g. Ask my friendly colleague to help me fix this mistake before my boss comes back into the office.)

However, as we learnt, the more focused you are on your goals day-to-day, the more quickly and easily you work towards them; the easier it also is to gain perspective and focus, and maintain motivation, when you encounter the really tough challenges.

Long-term important life goals

Your objective: To remember the bigger picture at all times for focus, perspective and motivation.

Dose: Immediately create your list and review it daily, or at least weekly, during your four-week plan.

How to: Use the 'Over To You' exercises on pages 22, 24 and 160.

Short-term four week plan goals

Your objective: To know which goals you are going to achieve during your four-week plan because then you will give yourself ample opportunity to train yourself into handling challenges with resilience *and* build your confidence.

Dose: Immediately create your list and review it daily, or at least near daily, during your four-week plan.

How to: Use the 'Over To You' exercise on page 167 to (a) help you decide what these goals are, (b) create a list of SMART goals for each one you want to achieve during your four week plan, and (c) add them to your planner so that you remember to do them. Examples of four week goals you might set before further defining them as SMART goals: reduce the number of arguments you and your spouse have by 80 per cent, become better able to handle criticism and use it to your advantage, becoming better at one particular element of your job, work out which lifelong career you want to change to, go on four first dates, learn a new skill, achieve a relationship goal, career goal or health and well-being goal.

Goals and goal setting
Your objective: To monitor and set goals you are driven to achieve and set them well.
Dose: As and when required.
How to: Use the 'Over To You' exercises on pages 159, 160 and 167.

Increasing motivation
Your objective: To keep motivation high to keep resilience high.
Dose: As and when required.
How to: Use the 'Over To You' exercise on page 168.

Remind yourself of past successes
Your objective: To keep self-belief high to keep resilience high.
Dose: As and when required.
How to: Use the 'Over To You' exercise on page 24.

Resilience Strengthening Habit 7:
Use problem-solving thoughts and behaviours

You MUST create and use your Resilience Pillar 1 statement
Your objective: To create a statement describing your self-serving, positive outlook on challenges (Resilience Pillar 1) and then affirm that outlook statement every time you encounter a challenge.
Dose: On day one of your four-week plan, create and rehearse your positive outlook statement and then, as and when

required, affirm that statement the very moment you encounter a challenge or even just think about your challenges.

How to: Use the first part of the 'Over To You' exercise on page 189.

You MUST problem-solve – Resilience Pillar 3
Your objective: To problem-solve relentlessly until you overcome your challenges, keep moving in the direction of your goals and achieve what you desperately want to achieve.

Dose: Daily, or near daily, to problem-solve, overcome challenges, achieve goals and regulate emotions.

How to: Use the second part of the 'Over To You' exercise on page 189.

Resilience Strengthening Habit 8:
Use intuition to make great decisions

Tune into your intuition for great decision making
Your objective: To use your intuition to help you make the right decisions for you.

Dose: As and when required.

How to: Use the 'Over To You' exercise on page 196.

Still Unknowingly Sabotaging Yourself?

Your resilience-o-meter will help you to check your resilience level anytime you want or need to (see pages 42–6). It will also help you to gauge if you are somehow sabotaging your ability to feel consistently resilient, or if someone else is.

During your four weeks, and thereafter, all you need to ask yourself when your resilience is low is:

◊ What can I do right now to help it to rise?
◊ What should I be doing, ongoing, to help it to stay high?

Use the chapter topics to do a quick check by asking yourself if your low resilience is due to your (1) thoughts, (2) emotions, (3) relationships, (4) self-care, (5) open chapters, (6) goal-setting, (7) problem-solving or (8) decision making. You can then use what you learnt in those chapters and the relevant 'Over To You' exercises to re-energise your resilience at any moment, e.g. 'I'm feeling fragile, I'll meet up with a loving friend'; 'I'm feeling low, I'll take a stroll in nature', 'I'm feeling stuck, I'll do some problem-solving to help me feel like I'm moving forward'; 'I'm feeling overwhelmed, I'll have a hot soak in the bath'; 'I'm feeling fatigued, I'll go to bed early'; etc.

Take resilience-o-meter readings for self-assessment and troubleshooting

Your objective: To be skilled at using your body to tell you how resilient you're feeling.

Dose: As and when required.

How to: Use the 'Over To You' exercise on page 45.

Determine why you lack resilience when Resilience Pillar 2 – a driving motivation – is present

Your objective: To identify anything knocking your resilience and adjust your daily habits and personalised four-week plan accordingly.

Dose: As and when required.

How to: Use the list on page 171 under 'Resilience Pillar 2 – A Driving Motivation – Must Be Present'.

Execute your Personalised Four-Week Plan

Well done for creating your personalised four-week plan! I'm proud of you! That's exactly the sort of proactive attitude and behaviour that is going to make you resilient in four weeks. Now clearly summarise your starting point and your end goal to programme in to your brain's 'sat nav' so your brain can go to work on it consciously and subconsciously.

Starting point:
The emotions I am currently feeling day-to-day are

....

The current issues/challenges I am experiencing are

....

Desired destination:
The emotions I want to feel by the end of four weeks are

....

The changes/improvements I would like to experience by the end of four weeks are

....

Example:
The emotions I am currently feeling day-to-day are:
◊ tired, insecure, and worried my marriage might end.
The current issues/challenges I am experiencing are:
◊ bickering with my spouse all the time, not feeling supported by them in pursuing my career, not giving enough time to the children.
The emotions I want to feel by the end of four weeks are:
◊ energetic, confident, optimistic my marriage will last and excited about my future.
The changes/improvements I would like to experience by the end of four weeks are:
◊ no bickering between me and my spouse and only occasional arguments, better practical and emotional support from my spouse, more quality time with the children.

Now it's time for you to work through your personalised four-week plan with focus and determination! This is what you need to do to become resilient in four weeks:

1. Take a resilience reading twice a day
2. Retrain your brain for resilience, every day
3. Carry out all resilience strengthening activities

1. Take a resilience reading twice a day

Start and end each day with a resilience-o-meter reading (page 45) so you can monitor your progress *and* stay focused on creating the resilient you during the first four weeks of your new, improved lifestyle. Note the date, whether it's morning or night, and the reading (level on your body).

The two daily readings will also help you monitor which activities help your daily resilience, which don't and what needs tweaking in your daily routine to reinforce your resilience armour. When your resilience-o-meter reading is low and you feel OFF (overwhelmed, fatigued or fragile), just ask yourself, 'Are my current thoughts and behaviours serving me and my goals and happiness or sabotaging me and my goals and happiness?' If they are self-serving, do them, if they are self-sabotaging stop doing them and choose self-serving thoughts and behaviours instead.

Remember, you can also take a resilience-o-meter reading at any time you want to check in with how resilient you're feeling so you can make good choices in that moment, e.g. 'Should I say yes to the extra workload?', 'Is this the best time for me to have that conversation with them?' or 'Do I need some me-time?'

2. Retrain your brain for resilience, every day

To retrain your brain to respond to every challenge with resilience, from today, meet every challenge you encounter with an immediate positive outlook on challenges (Resilience Pillar 1) immediately followed by problem-solving thoughts and behaviours (Resilience Pillar 3). Just remember these terms and employ them in quick succession:

1. **Notice challenge**
2. **Positive outlook**
3. **Problem-solve**

Write those three points on cards and place them around your house and/or office as reminders if you need to at the beginning, e.g. one by your bed and one on the fridge door.

Your thought-process will go something like this:

Step 1, Notice challenge: 'Whoa, this is a problem/challenge/obstacle.'

Step 2, Positive outlook: 'Challenges are good as they develop me and guide me towards my goals and happiness' or 'This obstacle serves me and my goals in some way'.

Step 3, Problem-solve: 'What can I learn from this challenge that will help me to achieve my end goals?'; 'How can I overcome this obstacle?'; 'What can I do right now to overcome this barrier?'; 'Who might be able to help me with this?'

3. Carry out all resilience strengthening activities in your personalised four-week plan

Ensure you do all the one-off and ongoing activities that you scheduled into your personalised four-week planner. Aim for a nightly review of your list of important long-term life goals and short-term four-week plan goals you want to achieve.

After You Create A Habit, It Becomes Fairly Automatic

For the next four weeks you are going to have to focus intently on creating a habit of resilience alongside the eight resilience strengthening habits that will help you. Once you have established your resilience habit with focus and purpose, your brain will take over, executing the thoughts and behaviours you have trained it into, fairly automatically, without much conscious thought on your part. Think of it like the difference between when you were learning how to drive a car (or learn some other skill) and once you'd become very proficient at it. If you do notice your newly formed habit slipping, simply come back to this section of the book and refresh your memory with this reference manual you have here.

Remember:

1. Only talk to yourself in positive words and with a focus on what can be rather than what has been, with a focus on goals rather than fears and desires rather than dislikes.

2. Do things daily, weekly and monthly that make you happy as an ongoing investment in your happiness, making you naturally more resilient minute-to-minute.

3. Cherish the good people in your life. They are priceless. Nurture the genuine, loving people who nurture healthy self-esteem and prune away the negative people who reinforce low self-worth.

4. Nurture and protect your body and mind. How you treat them both matters; your brain is paying attention. Be nice to yourself. Be your own best friend.

5. Guard the gates – your senses – from any unwelcome intruders.

6. Forgive yourself and others, or otherwise let go of the past, or else those things will drag you down forever, often entirely needlessly. It can take just moments to let go.

7. Set and pursue goals that really mean something to you; stop wasting your life on pursuits you don't care about.

8. Problem-solve your heart out because the answers always come eventually, and remember, you'll do most of this in your head as you go about your day-to-day life.

9. Always explore inwards for answers – often quick and correct ones that will help you solve life's puzzles and keep you moving towards your goals, happiness and life purpose.

Occasionally you might forget some of the good skills and habits we've spoken about in the book, but don't beat yourself up; it happens to the best of us! Simply dust yourself off and get back on track. It's *so* exciting to grow and develop and become a better version of ourselves.

Follow all the advice in this book, do it consistently and keep doing it. When you do, you'll notice how quick and easy training your brain for resilience is when you consciously and consistently respond to every challenge in a self-serving, thoughtful way.

It's time for you to reap the rewards of your new-found knowledge. Get serious about making the little, simple tweaks to your moment-to-moment habits and you'll transform your health and happiness.

Troubleshooting

'Obstacles don't have to stop you. If you run into a wall,
don't turn around and give up. Figure out how to climb it,
go through it, or work around it.' Michael Jordan

If you are getting stuck or feeling unsure about things, here are some questions you may have, with either the relevant chapters or other answers to help you.

Q. I'm struggling to snap out of negative thoughts and sometimes I obsess for hours over them. How can I stop?

A. It's important to distract yourself as soon as you realise you are doing it by focusing your attention on something else that makes you feel good. This might mean using a music playlist you've created, dancing, talking with a friend, etc. The longer you spend thinking negative thoughts, the more you are remoulding your brain to be good at feeling miserable. You might find it useful to quantify the effect of negative thoughts on your brain by comparing each ten minutes spent worrying to eating one chocolate bar. How many chocolate bars is it good for you to eat in one sitting? Also, revisit chapters: 'The Three Pillars of Resilience', 'Mind Your Attitude', 'The Power of Thinking', 'The Power of Emotions' and 'Caring for Ourselves'.

Q. I'm struggling to snap out of negative emotions. How can I?

A. Think about what you spend your minutes and days thinking about and doing and, if your thoughts and actions are self-sabotaging, channel your time and energy to self-serving thoughts and actions. What you repeatedly do will shape your life; it's up to you to choose better habits. What are you feeling glum about? Identify the source of your negative emotions and identify what you would rather feel and what you need to do to feel more consistently happy. If you are suppressing something you are unhappy about, it won't go away. Own your worth by proving to yourself that you are a valuable human being deserving of good fortune by doing something proactive about your happiness. Also, revisit chapters: 'The Three Pillars of Resilience', 'Mind Your Attitude', 'The Power of Thinking', 'The Power of Emotions' and 'Caring for Ourselves'.

Q. My partner/family aren't supporting me. How can I get them to?

A. Find out from them how you can gain the specific type of support that you want. Make any appropriate changes necessary that you agree with. Sometimes loved ones need reassurance that you are pursuing the right goals for the right reasons and that you are not going to waste time, money and energy on something fruitless. They may also be subconsciously concerned about what your choices may do to their time with you. Also, revisit chapters: 'Caring for Ourselves', 'Positive Relationships' and 'CreativeProblem-Solving'.

Q. I'm struggling to overcome a tragedy. What can I do?

A. Firstly, know that time really is a great healer. Allow yourself to feel the pain, rather than suppress it, but equally don't let your whole day every day be about that. Get busy; focus your time on worthwhile things. What goals do you want to achieve and what can you do now to move you in that direction? The rear-view mirror is for quick glances; if you keep focusing on it, you will have accidents. Focusing on future goals helps you to channel your energy in a pleasant direction rather than a painful one. You must indulge self-care: make it a daily pleasure if you need to and make it different every day or every other day so you don't become immune to its effects. Seek out people who are worse off than you in some way whom you can help, and help them. That might be by volunteering at a charity, handing warm food out to the homeless in your local town or city, or helping out a friend, colleague or neighbour. If there is a message the tragedy has made you want to share with the world, share it; it will help you to feel the tragedy has served a bigger purpose somehow. Also, revisit chapters: 'The Three Pillars Of Resilience', 'Mind Your Attitude', 'The Power of Thinking', 'The Power of Emotions', 'Positive Relationships' and 'Caring for Ourselves'.

Q. I'm struggling with problem-solving. How can I be better?

A. Use the strategies in the chapter 'Creative Problem-Solving' and ask family, friends or a professional to help. Persistence is also key. It might be that you are struggling to problem-solve because you don't have a genuine motivation. Reassess what you're working towards; it might just need a slight tweak to get you truly motivated and energetically problem-solving with ease. Tune in to that internal ease of energy flow or lack thereof. What's making it feel a bit like trudging through treacle? Do you have any concerns about what you're pursuing? Maybe something is purposefully holding you back, subconsciously, that you need to recognise. Also, revisit chapters: 'Setting Goals for Proper Motivation', 'Creative Problem-Solving' and 'Intuitive Decision-Making'.

Q. I'm struggling with motivation. How can I solve this?

A. Look at why you are pursuing this/these goal(s). A good question to ask yourself is, 'If I could do anything (pursue any goal) in this field, what would it be?' Sometimes we set goals based on parameters we think we *should* meet. Build your career and relationships around your personality, not the other way around. Build your life around who you are at your core. Also, revisit chapters: 'The Three Pillars of Resilience', 'Mind Your Attitude', 'Setting Goals for Proper Motivation' and 'Intuitive Decision-Making'.

Q. I'm feeling overwhelmed. What can I do?

A. Indulge self-care, seek help from significant others, or seek out a resilient group or a professional if you have nobody to call upon. Re-evaluate every task you've taken on and remove what's not necessary or delay what can wait, giving you more focus and energy for the important tasks before you right now. Remove distractions: that might mean temporarily removing emails or social media from your mobile phone so they're not as accessible. Also, revisit chapters: 'The Three Pillars of Resilience', 'The Power of Thinking', 'The Power of Emotions', 'Positive Relationships', 'Caring for Ourselves' and 'Setting Goals for Proper Motivation'.

Q. I'm feeling exhausted. What can I do?

A. Assess why you are exhausted; is it your thoughts or your actions or non-true goals you're pursuing that are exhausting you? Taking time out is paramount, as is re-evaluating everything in your schedule and, albeit temporarily, removing what doesn't need to be on there right now to conserve your energy. Indulge proper self-care by resting your body and your brain. Also, revisit chapters: 'The Three Pillars of Resilience', 'Mind Your Attitude', 'The Power of Thinking', 'The Power of Emotions', 'Positive Relationships', 'Caring for Ourselves' and 'Setting Goals for Proper Motivation'.

Q. I feel clouded in my judgements. What should I do?

A. Seek help from loved ones, correctly label your negative emotions, focus on emotion-regulation strategies, and focus on what you want, i.e. your goals. Reflect and introspect on whether you can obtain your desired goals from the people and/or lifestyle you have and if not, make the necessary changes. It's possible there is something you are trying to ignore or suppress. Give your brain and body credit for knowing things and find out what they are reacting to. Then do something about it so the clouds disappear. Make sure you frequently exercise, to help you gain clarity, and mix up your routine to help refocus your view and your thoughts. Also, revisit chapters: 'The Power of Thinking', 'The Power of Emotions', 'Positive Relationships', 'Caring for Ourselves', 'Creative Problem-Solving' and 'Intuitive Decision-Making'.

Q. I'm struggling to move on from someone or something. How do I?

A. Stop wasting your life on the wrong people and worrying about what has happened. Only focus on the things you want from your future, set realistic goals, and problem-solve how you're going to achieve them. Every past relationship and event is a fantastic learning curve that teaches us what we want, what we don't want, what we're willing to put up with and what we're not willing to put up with. Use that to excitedly define what sort of relationship(s) and experiences you do want from your future. Also, revisit chapters: 'The Three Pillars of Resilience', 'Mind Your Attitude', 'Positive Relationships', 'Caring for Ourselves', 'Setting Goals for Proper Motivation', 'Creative Problem-Solving' and 'Intuitive Decision-Making'.

Q. I've been made redundant and it's knocked my confidence. What would you suggest?

A. First, even if it was your dream job, look for what you can do next that will make you even happier; either a new job or career, or which goals they can help you achieve, like a new car or an investment in your future. Second, take whatever learning you can from the experience. If you did make mistakes, you probably won't make them again and that might help you to achieve a much more important goal and lots of happiness in your future. Learning from our mistakes helps us achieve goals and be happy in our future. Also, revisit chapters: 'The Three Pillars of Resilience', 'Mind Your Attitude', 'Caring for Ourselves', 'Setting Goals for Proper Motivation', 'Creative Problem-Solving' and 'Intuitive Decision-Making'.

Q. My spouse and I are arguing all the time. I'm so worried that I'm struggling to talk about it. What should I do?

A. When you focus on the fears, you will work towards the fears, so rather than thinking, 'What if we separate or divorce or just have a loveless marriage?', find out (problem-solve) what you're both dissatisfied with and how you will tweak things to solve each other's issues. Always talk in terms of what you do want, not what you don't want. Marriage is a daily commitment to love and cherish that person who has opted to spend their entire life with you. There are going to be ups and downs but the downs should steadily reduce over time, so use each challenge as an opportunity to prevent it from occurring again. Also, revisit chapters: 'Positive Relationships', 'Caring for Ourselves', 'Setting Goals for Proper Motivation', 'Creative Problem-Solving' and 'Intuitive Decision-Making'.

⊱— FINAL NOTE —⊰

Big changes can happen in a very short space of time.

Live in the moment and steer your life as you want to. You're already steering it anyway, so you may as well wake up and steer it in the direction you actually want to go in: a happy, fulfilling direction.

Look after yourself mentally and physically. When you do, you benefit and mankind benefits, too. We are connected and we affect one another.

Keep a copy of this book handy, rather than lending it out, so that you can reread it in its entirety or selectively, as and when you need to refocus and remind yourself of all the information and tools to create and maintain the relentlessly resilient you.

I know you can easily achieve the newly refined resilient you in four weeks or less. Now make small, simple tweaks to your daily habits and go and be the person you are so capable of being.

References

1. Lieberman, M. D., Eisenberger, N. I., Crockett, M. J., Tom, S. M., Pfeifer, J. H. and Way, B. M. (2007). 'Putting Feelings Into Words: Affect Labeling Disrupts Amygdala Activity in Response to Affective Stimuli', *Psychological Science*, 18(5): 421–8.

2. Blackwell, L. S., Trzesniewski, K. H. and Dweck, C. S. (2007). 'Implicit Theories of Intelligence Predict Achievement Across an Adolescent Transition: A Longitudinal Study and an Intervention', *Child Development*, 78(1): 246–63.

3. Elliott, R., Zahn, R., Deakin, J. F. W. and Anderson, I. M. (2011). 'Affective Cognition and its Disruption in Mood Disorders', *Neuropsychopharmacology*, 36(1): 153–82.

4. Fazio, R. H. and Olson, M. A. (2014). 'The MODE Model: Attitude-Behavior Processes as a Function of Motivation and Opportunity', in Sherman, J. W., Gawronski, B. and Trope, Y. (eds) *Dual-Process Theories of the Social Mind*, New York: Guilford Press, pp. 155–71.

5. Scinta, A. and Gable, S. L. (2007). 'Automatic and Self-Reported Attitudes in Romantic Relationships', *Personality and Social Psychology Bulletin*, 33(7): 1008–22.

6. Hölzel, B. K., Carmody, J., Vangel, M., Congleton, C., Yerramsetti, S. M., Gard, T. and Lazar, S. W. (2011). 'Mindfulness Practice Leads to Increases in Regional Brain Gray Matter Density', *Psychiatry Research: Neuroimaging*, 191(1): 36–43.

7. Hölzel, B. K., Carmody, J., Evans, K. C., Hoge, E. A., Dusek, J. A., Morgan, L., Pitman, R. K. and Lazar, S. W. (2010). 'Stress Reduction Correlates with Structural Changes in the Amygdala', *Social Cognitive and Affective Neuroscience*, 5(1): 11–17.

8. Newberg, A. and Waldman, M. R. (2012). *Words Can Change Your Brain: 12 Conversation Strategies to Build Trust, Resolve Conflict, and Increase Intimacy*, New York: Avery.

9. Doidge, N. (2006). *The Brain That Changes Itself: Stories of Personal Triumph from the Frontiers of Brain Science*, New York: Penguin Group.

10. Pascual-Leone, A., Amedi, A., Fregni, F. and Merabet, L. B. (2005). 'The Plastic Human Brain Cortex', *Annual Review of Neuroscience*, 28: 377–401.

11. Hatzigeorgiadis, A., Zourbanos, N., Galanis, E. and Theodorakis, Y. (2011). 'Self-Talk and Sports Performance: A Meta-Analysis', *Perspectives on Psychological Science*, 6(4): 348–56.

12. Hatzigeorgiadis, A., Zourbanos, N., Mpoumpaki, S. and Theodorakis, Y. (2009). 'Mechanisms Underlying the Self-Talk–Performance Relationship: The Effects of Self-Talk on Self-Confidence and Anxiety', *Psychology of Sport and Exercise*, 10(1): 186–92.

13. Lane, A. M., Totterdell, P., MacDonald, I., Devonport, T. J., Friesen, A. P., Beedie, C. J., Stanley, D. and Nevill, A. (2016). 'Brief Online Training Enhances Competitive Performance: Findings of the BBC Lab UK Psychological Skills Intervention Study', *Frontiers in Psychology*, 7.
   Available at: http://journal.frontiersin.org/article/10.3389/fpsyg.2016.00413/full

14. St Clair Gibson, A. and Foster, C. (2007). The Role of Self-Talk in the Awareness of Physiological State and Physical Performance', *Sports Medicine*, 37(12): 1029–44.

15. Longe, O., Maratos, F. A., Gilbert, P., Evans, G., Volker, F., Rockliff, H. and Rippon, G. (2010). 'Having a Word with Yourself: Neural Correlates of Self-Criticism and Self-Reassurance', *Neuroimage*, 49(2): 1849–56.

16. Araki, K., Mintah, J. K., Mack, M. G., Huddleston, S., Larson, L. and Jacobs, K. (2006). 'Belief in Self-Talk and Dynamic Balance Performance', *Athletic Insight: The Online Journal of Sport Psychology*, 8(4).
   Available at: http://athleticinsight.com/Vol8Iss4/SelfTalkPDF.pdf

17. Cohn, M. A., Fredrickson, B. L., Brown, S. L., Mikels, J. A. and Conway, A. M. (2009). 'Happiness Unpacked: Positive Emotions Increase Life Satisfaction by Building Resilience', *Emotion*, 9(3): 361–8.

18. Tugade, M. M. and Fredrickson, B. L. (2004). 'Resilient Individuals Use Positive Emotions to Bounce Back From Negative Emotional Experiences', *Journal of Personality and Social Psychology*, 86(2): 320–33.

19. Kuhbandner, C., Lichtenfeld, S. and Pekrun, R. (2011). 'Always Look on the Broad Side of Life: Happiness Increases the Breadth of Sensory Memory', *Emotion*, 11(4): 958-64.

20. Fredrickson, B. L. and Branigan, C. (2005). 'Positive Emotions Broaden the Scope of Attention and Thought-Action Repertoires', *Cognition and Emotion*, 19(3): 313–32.

21. Galatzer-Levy, I. R., Brown, A. D., Henn-Haase, C., Metzler, T. J., Neylan, T. C. and Marmar, C. R. (2013). 'Positive and Negative Emotion Prospectively Predict Trajectories of Resilience and Distress among High-Exposure Police Officers', *Emotion*, 13(3): 545–53.

22. Dennis, T. A. and Hajcak, G. (2009). 'The Late Positive Potential: A Neurophysiological Marker for Emotion Regulation in Children', *Journal of Child Psychology and Psychiatry*, 50(11): 1373–83.

23. Gross, J. J. and John, O. P. (2003). 'Individual Differences in Two Emotion Regulation Processes: Implications for Affect, Relationships, and Well-Being', *Journal of Personality and Social Psychology*, 85(2): 348–62.

24. Hajcak, G. and Nieuwenhuis, S. (2006). 'Reappraisal Modulates the Electrocortical Response to Unpleasant Pictures', *Cognitive, Affective, & Behavioral Neuroscience*, 6(4): 291–7.

25. Kalokerinos, E. K., Greenaway, K. H. and Denson, T. F. (2015). 'Reappraisal but not Suppression Downregulates the Experience of Positive and Negative Emotion', *Emotion*, 15(3): 271–5.

26. Hajcak, G., Dunning, J. P. and Foti, D. (2009). 'Motivated and Controlled Attention to Emotion: Time-Course of the Late Positive Potential', *Clinical Neurophysiology*, 120(3): 505–10.

27. Quoidbach, J., Gross, J. J. and Mikolajczak, M. (2015). 'Positive Interventions: An Emotion Regulation Perspective', *Psychological Bulletin*, 141(3): 655–93.

28. Lyubomirsky, S. and Layous, K. (2013). 'How Do Simple Positive Activities Increase Well-Being?', *Current Directions in Psychological Science*, 22(1): 57–62.

29. Lyubomirsky, S., Sheldon, K. M. and Schkade, D. (2005). 'Pursuing Happiness: The Architecture of Sustainable Change', *Review of General Psychology*, 9(2): 111–31.

30. Sheldon, K. M., Boehm, J. K. and Lyubomirsky, S. (2012). 'Variety is the Spice of Happiness: The Hedonic Adaptation Prevention Model', in David, S., Bonnywell, I. and Ayers, A. C. (eds) *Oxford Handbook of Happiness*, Oxford: Oxford University Press, pp. 901–14.

31. Emmons, R. A. and McCullough, M. E. (2003). 'Counting Blessings Versus Burdens: An Experimental Investigation of Gratitude and Subjective Well-Being in Daily Life', *Journal of Personality and Social Psychology*, 84(2): 377–89.

32. Ulrich, R. S., Simons, R. F., Losito, B. D., Fiorito, E., Miles, M. A. and Zelson, M. (1991). 'Stress Recovery during Exposure to Natural and Urban Environments', *Journal of Environmental Psychology*, 11(3): 201–30.

33. Berry, M. S., Sweeney, M. M., Morath, J., Odum, A. L. and Jordan, K. E. (2014). 'The Nature of Impulsivity: Visual Exposure to Natural Environments Decreases Impulsive Decision-Making in a Delay Discounting Task', *PLOS ONE*, 9.
    Available at: http://journals.plos.org/plosone/article?id=10.1371/journal.pone.0097915

34. Gruber, J., Kogan, A., Quoidbach, J. and Mauss, I. B. (2013). 'Happiness Is Best Kept Stable: Positive Emotion Variability Is Associated With Poorer Psychological Health', *Emotion*, 13(1): 1–6.

35. Powell, A. (2012). 'Decoding Keys to a Healthy Life', USA: *Harvard Gazette*.
    Available at: http://news.harvard.edu/gazette/story/2012/02/decoding-keys-to-a-healthy-life/

36. Shenk, J. W. (2009). 'What Makes Us Happy?', USA: *The Atlantic*.

Available at: http://www.theatlantic.com/magazine/archive/2009/06/
what-makes-us-happy/307439/

37. Waldinger, R. (2015). 'What Makes a Good Life? Lessons from the Longest Study on
Happiness', USA: TED Conferences.
Available at: http://www.ted.com/talks/robert_waldinger_what_makes_a_
good_life_lessons_from_the_longest_study_on_happiness/transcript?language=en

38. Powell, A. 'Decoding keys to a healthy life'.

39. Graber, R., Turner, R. and Madill, A. (2016). 'Best Friends and Better Coping:
Facilitating Psychological Resilience through Boys' and Girls' Closest Friendships',
British Journal of Psychology, 107(2): 338–58.

40. Lyons, A. and Heywood, W. (2016). 'Collective Resilience as a Protective Factor for
the Mental Health and Well-Being of HIV-Positive Gay Men', *Psychology of Sexual
Orientation and Gender Diversity*, 3(4): 473–9.

41. Holt-Lunstad, J., Smith, T. B., Baker, M., Harris, T. and Stephenson, D. (2015).
'Loneliness and Social Isolation as Risk Factors for Mortality: A Meta-Analytic
Review', *Perspectives on Psychological Science*, 10(2): 227–37.

42. Cohen, S. (2004). 'Social Relationships and Health', *American Psychologist*, 59(8):
676–84.

43. Waldinger, R. J. and Schulz, M. S. (2010). 'What's Love Got To Do With It? Social
Functioning, Perceived Health, and Daily Happiness in Married Octogenarians',
Psychology and Aging, 25(2), 422–31.

44. Aknin, L. B., Broesch, T., Hamlin, J. K. and Van de Vondervoort, J. W. (2015).
'Prosocial Behavior Leads to Happiness in a Small-Scale Rural Society', *Journal of
Experimental Psychology: General*, 144(4): 788–95.

45. Alessi, E. J. (2016). 'Resilience in sexual and gender minority forced migrants: A quali-
tative exploration', *Traumatology*, 22(3): 203–13.

46. Gledhill, R. (2013). 'Muslims "Are Britain's Top Charity Givers"', UK: *The Times*.
Available at: http://www.thetimes.co.uk/tto/faith/article3820522.ece [Paywall]

47. Piferi, R. L. and Lawler, K. A. (2006). 'Social Support and Ambulatory Blood
Pressure: An Examination of both Receiving and Giving', *International Journal of
Psychophysiology*, 62(2): 328–36.

48. Wahrendorf, M., Ribet, C., Zins, M., Goldberg, M. and Siegrist, J. (2010). 'Perceived
Reciprocity in Social Exchange and Health Functioning in Early Old Age: Prospective
Findings from the GAZEL Study', *Aging and Mental Health*, 14(4): 425–32.

49. Ahmad, M. H., Shahar, S., Teng, N. I., Manaf, Z.A., Sakian, N.I. and Omar, B. (2014).
'Applying Theory of Planned Behavior to Predict Exercise Maintenance in Sarcopenic
Elderly', *Clinical Interventions in Aging*, 9: 1551–61.

50. Sheppard, B. H., Hartwick, J. and Warshaw, P. R. (1988). 'The Theory of Reasoned Action: A Meta-Analysis of Past Research with Recommendations for Modifications and Future Research', *Journal of Consumer Research*, 15(3): 325–43.

51. Tarkiainen, A. and Sundqvist, S. (2005). 'Subjective Norms, Attitudes and Intentions of Finnish Consumers in Buying Organic Food', *British Food Journal*, 107(11): 808–22.

52. Field, T. (1996). 'Attachment and Separation in Young Children', *Annual Review of Psychology*, 47:541–61.

53. Harris, J. R. (1998). *The Nurture Assumption: Why Children Turn Out The Way They Do*, New York: Free Press.

54. Kirkpatrick, L. A. and Hazan, C. (1994). 'Attachment Styles and Close Relationships: A Four-Year Prospective Study', *Personal Relationships*, 1(2): 123–42.

55. Fraley, R. C. (2010). 'A Brief Overview of Adult Attachment Theory and Research', USA: University of Illinois.
    Available at: https://internal.psychology.illinois.edu/~rcfraley/attachment.htm

56. Fraley, R. C. and Shaver, P. R. (2000). 'Adult Romantic Attachment: Theoretical Developments, Emerging Controversies, and Unanswered Questions', *Review of General Psychology*, 4(2): 132–54.

57. Roberts, J. E., Gotlib, I. H. and Kassel, J. D. (1996). 'Adult Attachment Security and Symptoms of Depression: The Mediating Roles of Dysfunctional Attitudes and Low Self-Esteem', *Journal of Personality and Social Psychology*, 70 (2): 310–20.

58. Roberts, R. E. L. and Bengtson, V. L. (1993). 'Relationships with Parents, Self-Esteem, and Psychological Well-Being in Young Adulthood', *Social Psychology Quarterly*. 56(4): 263–77.

59. Neff, K. D. and Beretvas, S. N. (2013). 'The Role of Self-Compassion in Romantic Relationships', *Self and Identity*, 12(1): 78–98.

60. Hegberg, N. J. and Tone, E. B. (2014). 'Physical Activity and Stress Resilience: Considering those At-Risk for Developing Mental Health Problems', *Mental Health and Physical Activity*, 8: 1–7.

61. Schoenfeld, T. J., Rada, P., Pieruzzini, P. R., Hsueh, B. and Gould, E. (2013). 'Physical Exercise Prevents Stress-Induced Activation of Granule Neurons and Enhances Local Inhibitory Mechanisms in the Dentate Gyrus', *Journal of Neuroscience*, 33(18): 7770–7.

62. McAuley, E., Blissmer, B., Katula, J., Duncan, T. E. and Mihalko, S. L. (2000). 'Physical Activity, Self-Esteem, and Self-Efficacy Relationships in Older Adults: A Randomized Controlled Trial', *Annals of Behavioral Medicine*, 22(2): 131–9.

63. McAuley, E., Elavsky, S., Motl, R. W., Konopack, J. F., Hu, L. and Marquez, D. X. (2005). 'Physical Activity, Self-Efficacy, and Self-Esteem: Longitudinal Relationships in Older Adults', *The Journals of Gerontology: Series B*, 60 (5): 268–75.

64. Dunn, A. L., Trivedi, M. H., Kampert, J. B., Clark, C. G. and Chambliss, H. O. (2005). 'Exercise Treatment for Depression: Efficacy and Dose Response', *American Journal of Preventive Medicine*, 28(1): 1–8.

65. Thomas, A. G., Dennis, A., Bandettini, P. A. and Johansen-Berg, H. (2012). 'The Effects of Aerobic Activity on Brain Structure', *Frontiers in Psychology*, 3(86): 1–9.

66. Vaynman, S. and Gomez-Pinilla, F. (2005). 'License to Run: Exercise Impacts Functional Plasticity in the Intact and Injured Central Nervous System by Using Neurotrophins', *Neurorehabilitation and Neural Repair*, 19(4): 283–95.

67. Patten, A. R., Yau, S. U., Fontaine, C. J., Meconi, A., Wortman, R. C. and Christie, B. R. (2015). 'The Benefits of Exercise on Structural and Functional Plasticity in the Rodent Hippocampus of Different Disease Models', *Brain Plasticity*, 1(1): 93–123.

68. Venkatraman, V., Huettel, S. A., Chuah, L. Y. M., Payne, J. W. and Chee, M. W. L. (2011). 'Sleep Deprivation Biases the Neural Mechanisms Underlying Economic Preferences', *Journal of Neuroscience*, 31(10): 3712–18.

69. Minkel, J., Htaik, O., Banks, S. and Dinges, D. (2011). 'Emotional Expressiveness in Sleep-Deprived Healthy Adults', *Behavioural Sleep Medicine*, 9(1): 5–14.

70. Van der Helm, E. and Walker, M. P. (2009). 'Overnight Therapy? The Role of Sleep in Emotional Brain Processing', *Psychological Bulletin*, 135(5): 731–48.

71. Yoo, S. S., Gujar, N., Hu, P., Jolesz, F. A. and Walker, M. P. (2007). 'The Human Emotional Brain Without Sleep – A Prefrontal Amygdala Disconnect', *Current Biology*, 17(20): 877–8.

72. Lee, S. W. S. and Schwarz, N. (2011). 'Wiping the Slate Clean: Psychological Consequences of Physical Cleansing', *Current Directions in Psychological Science*, 20(5): 307–11.

73. Schnall, S., Haidt, J., Clore, G. L. and Jordan, A. H. (2008). 'Disgust as Embodied Moral Judgment', *Personality and Social Psychology Bulletin*, 34(8): 1096–109.

74. Holland, R. W., Hendriks, M. and Aarts, H. (2005). 'Smells like Clean Spirit: Nonconscious Effects of Scent on Cognition and Behavior', *Psychological Science*, 16(9): 689–93.

75. SOASTA (2013). 'SOASTA Survey: What App Do You Check First in the Morning?' USA: SOASTA.
    Available at: https://www.soasta.com/press-releases/soasta-survey-what-app-do-you-check-first-in-the-morning

76. Kross, E., Verduyn, P., Demiralp, E., Park, J., Lee, D. S., Lin, N., Shablack, H., Jonides, J. and Ybarra, O. (2013). 'Facebook Use Predicts Declines in Subjective Well-Being in Young Adults', *PLOS ONE*, 8(8).
    Available at: http://journals.plos.org/plosone/article?id=10.1371/journal.pone.0069841

77. Hamid, A. A., Pettibone, J. R., Mabrouk, O. S., Hetrick, V. L., Schmidt, R., Vander Weele, C. M., Kennedy, R. T., Aragona, B. J. and Berke, J. D. (2016). 'Mesolimbic Dopamine Signals the Value of Work', *Nature Neuroscience*, 19(1): 117–26.

78. Locke, E. A. and Latham, G. P. (2002). 'Building a Practically Useful Theory of Goal Setting and Task Motivation: A 35-Year Odyssey', *American Psychologist*, 57(9): 705–17.

79. Locke, E. A., Shaw, K. N., Saari, L. M. and Latham, G. P. (1981). 'Goal Setting and Task Performance: 1969–1980', *Psychological Bulletin*, 90(1): 125–52.

80. Ibid.

81. Gollwitzer, P. M. and Brandstätter, V. (1997). 'Implementation Intentions and Effective Goal Pursuit', *Journal of Personality and Social Psychology*, 73(1): 186–99.

82. Latham, G. P. and Locke, E. A. (2007). 'New Developments in and Directions for Goal-Setting Research', *European Psychologist*, 12(4): 290–300.

83. Stickgold, R. and Ellenbogen, J. M. (2008). 'Sleep on It: How Snoozing Makes You Smarter', *Scientific American Mind*, August: 23–29.

84. Osborn, A. (1953). *Applied Imagination: Principles and Procedures of Creative Problem-Solving*, New York: Creative Education Foundation Press.

85. Oppezzo, M. and Schwartz, D. L. (2014). 'Give Your Ideas Some Legs: The Positive Effect of Walking on Creative Thinking', *Journal of Experimental Psychology: Learning, Memory, and Cognition*, 40(4): 1142–52.

86. Förster, J., Friedman, R. S. and Liberman, N. (2004). 'Temporal Construal Effects on Abstract and Concrete Thinking: Consequences for Insight and Creative Cognition', *Journal of Personality and Social Psychology*, 87(2): 177–89.

87. Christoff, K., Gordon, A. M., Smallwood, J., Smith, R. and Schooler, J. W. (2009). 'Experience Sampling During fMRI Reveals Default Network and Executive System Contributions to Mind Wandering', *Proceedings of the National Academy of Sciences of the United States of America*, 106 (21): 8719–24.

88. Isen, A. M., Daubman, K. A. and Nowicki, G. P. (1987). 'Positive Affect Facilitates Creative Problem Solving', *Journal of Personality and Social Psychology*, 52(6): 1122–31.

89. Wagner, U., Gais, S., Haider, H., Verleger, R. and Born, J. (2004). 'Sleep Inspires Insight', *Nature*, 427: 352–5.

90. Horne, J. A. (1988). 'Sleep Loss and "Divergent" Thinking Ability', *Sleep*, 11(6): 528–36.

91. Soon, C. S., Brass, M., Heinze, H. J. and Haynes, J. D. (2008). 'Unconscious Determinants of Free Decisions in the Human Brain', *Nature Neuroscience*, 11(5): 543–5.

92. Hodgkinson, G.P., Langan-Fox, J. and Sadler-Smith, E. (2008). 'Intuition: A Fundamental Bridging Construct in the Behavioural Sciences', *British Journal of Psychology*, 99(1): 1–27.

93. HeartMath Institute (2012). 'Heart Intelligence', USA: HeartMath Institute. Available at: https://www.heartmath.org/articles-of-the-heart/ the-math-of-heartmath/heart-intelligence/

94. McCraty, R., Atkinson, M., Tomasino, D. and Tiller, W. A. (1998). 'The Electricity of Touch: Detection and Measurement of Cardiac Energy Exchange Between People', in Pribram, K. H. (ed.) *Brain and Values: Is a Biological Science of Values Possible?* Mahwah, NJ: Lawrence Erlbaum Associates, pp. 359–79.

95. McCraty, R., Deyhle, A. and Childre, D. (2012). 'The Global Coherence Initiative: Creating a Coherent Planetary Standing Wave', *Global Advances in Health and Medicine*, 1(1): 64–77.

96. Voss, J. L. and Paller, K. A. (2009). 'An Electrophysiological Signature of Unconscious Recognition Memory', *Nature Neuroscience*, 12(3): 349–55.

97. Bechara, A., Damasio, H., Tranel, D. and Damasio, A. R. (1997). 'Deciding Advantageously Before Knowing the Advantageous Strategy', *Science*, 275(5304): 1293–5.

98. Lufityanto, G., Donkin, C. and Pearson, J. (2016). 'Measuring Intuition: Nonconscious Emotional Information Boosts Decision Accuracy and Confidence', *Psychological Science*, 27(5): 622–34.

99. Association for Psychological Science. 'Intuition – It's More Than a Feeling', USA: Association for Psychological Science. Available at: https://www.psychologicalscience.org/news/minds-business/ intuition-its-more-than-a-feeling.html

100. McCraty, R., Atkinson, M. and Bradley, R. T. (2004). 'Electrophysiological Evidence of Intuition: Part 1. The Surprising Role of the Heart', *Journal of Alternative and Complementary Medicine*, 10(1): 133–43.

101. Rezaei, S., Mirzaei, M. and Zali, M. R. (2014). 'Nonlocal Intuition: Replication and Paired-Subjects Enhancement Effects', *Global Advances in Health and Medicine*, 3(2): 5–15.

102. McCraty, R. and Atkinson, M. (2014). 'Electrophysiology of Intuition: Pre-Stimulus Responses in Group and Individual Participants Using a Roulette Paradigm', *Global Advances in Health and Medicine*, 3(2): 16–27.

103. Bradley, R. T. (2007). 'The Language of Entrepreneurship: Energetic Information Processing in Entrepreneurial Decision and Action', USA: HeartMath Institute. Available at: https://www.heartmath.org/assets/uploads/2015/01/ language-of-entrepreneurship.pdf

104. HeartMath Institute. 'The Importance of Heart Rate Variability on Our Emotional Health and Well-Being', USA: HeartMath Institute.
Available at: https://www.heartmath.com/blog/articles/hrv-emotional-health-well-being-vanderkolk/

Acknowledgements

This book, whilst dedicated to my nearest and dearest, was only made possible with the support and belief of those around me who helped make this book a reality.

I first want to say a massive thank you to all of my sweet, giving clients who gave me permission to share some of their stories within this book, under aliases, and for liaising with me to ensure all details were correct. The generosity and encouragement they have shown me is truly humbling and I will always remember it as we make our journeys together. I also want to thank all of my coaching clients for allowing me into their personal lives and entrusting me to help them, all of which has made this book possible.

I also want to sincerely thank the professionals who have helped me to be sitting here writing this. Firstly, my talent agency for believing in me and helping me to realise my dreams of publishing with one of the 'big five'. Secondly, my publisher for believing in me enough from day one to offer me a three-book publishing deal. Thirdly, my editor for so skilfully and compassionately helping me to develop myself as a writer and helping the book become what it is today.

Then, of course, there is the support system that keeps you sane and, in my case, that was first and foremost my husband. From taking on more household chores and ensuring I ate properly to still smiling at me when I was moody and miserable from the pressures of deadlines, to coaching me when I needed support and being excited with me as the book progressed, to always supporting my absences as I spent my time researching and writing and forcing me to take breaks to prevent burnout. His unrelenting love and support is one of the reasons he is such an amazing husband but also undoubtedly one of the reasons this writing journey went as smoothly as it did.

Lastly, I do want to say a final thank you to all those who have ever vocalised their belief in me, especially my amazing parents. I believe this is truly one of the greatest gifts you can give any human being, for those words can resonate for decades and those sentiments from others definitely helped me to continue believing in myself.

Thank you so, so much, all of you. xx